THE BASEBALL HALL OF SHAME'S
WARPED RECORD BOOK

D0179728

The Baseball Hall of Shame's
WARPED RECORD BOOK

BRUCE NASH AND ALLAN ZULLO

BOB SMITH, CURATOR

Collier Books

Macmillan Publishing Company NEW YORK

Maxwell Macmillan Canada TORONTO

Maxwell Macmillan International

NEW YORK OXFORD SINGAPORE SYDNEY

Copyright © 1991 by Nash & Zullo Productions, Inc.

All rights reserved. No part of this book may be reproduced or transmitted in any form or by any means, electronic or mechanical, including photocopying, recording, or by any information storage and retrieval system, without permission in writing from the Publisher.

Collier Books

Macmillan Publishing Company

866 Third Avenue

New York, NY 10022

Maxwell Macmillan Canada, Inc.

1200 Eglinton Avenue East

Suite 200

Don Mills, Ontario M3C 3N1

Macmillan Publishing Company is part of the Maxwell Communication Group of Companies.

Library of Congress Cataloging-in-Publication Data

Nash, Bruce M.
    The Baseball Hall of Shame's warped record book/by Bruce Nash and Allan Zullo; Bob Smith, curator.—1st Collier Books ed.
        p.   cm.
    ISBN 0-02-029485-9
    1. Baseball—United States—Anecdotes. 2. Baseball—United States—Records. I. Zullo, Allan. II. Smith, Bob. III. Title.
    GV863.A1N365 1991   91-14481 CIP
    796.357'0973—dc20

Macmillan books are available at special discounts for bulk purchases for sales promotions, premiums, fund-raising, or educational use. For details, contact:

                    Special Sales Director
                    Macmillan Publishing Company
                    866 Third Avenue
                    New York, NY 10022

First Collier Books Edition 1991

10 9 8 7 6 5 4 3 .

Printed in the United States of America

To my friend Adam Shapiro, who, like this book, makes me laugh and not take life too seriously.

—B.N.

To my friend Dave Haglund, who not only follows the beat of a different drummer, but truly is a different drummer—and a damn good one, too.

—A.Z.

To Ann, who stood by me through the tough times.

—B.S.

Contents

Acknowledgments

We wish to thank those players, coaches, and umpires who shared a few laughs with us as they recounted the inglorious moments that earned them a niche in *The Baseball Hall of Shame's Warped Record Book*.

This book couldn't have been completed without the assistance and cooperation of the National Baseball Hall of Fame Library in Cooperstown, New York. We especially appreciate the help, guidance, and friendship of senior research associate Bill Deane. We are grateful for the invaluable research provided by J. Mark Sweeney of the Library of Congress in Washington, D.C. Our thanks also extend to our good friend and reporter Bernie Ward for his help in documenting the warped records.

We wish to acknowledge the assistance of Paul Adomites; Morris Eckhouse, executive director of the Society for American Baseball Research (SABR); Paul Haas, Sports Books, etc.; Bee Hanks, Phenom Sports; Tot Holmes, Holmes Publishing; Tom Macsinka; Court

Michelson; Bobby Plapinger, Baseball Books; Richard Topp, president of SABR; and Guy Waterman.

And a very special thanks go to our two favorite stars, Sophie Nash and Kathy Zullo.

Many of today's older teams had different names in the 1890s and the early part of this century. In recounting records that occurred back then, we refer to these teams by their current names rather than their past monikers to avoid confusion.

B.N.

A.Z.

For the Record

After chronicling hundreds of wacky, crazy, and incredible but true stories in four volumes of *The Baseball Hall of Shame*, we decided to produce a record book like no other ever published.

Let's face it. Most record books have one thing in common—they're boring! They're filled with nothing but bland statistics that could put an insomniac to sleep. They have no pizazz, no fun, no humor.

We figured that fans were ready for an entirely different, off-the-wall record book—one chock-full of hundreds of zany achievements. So we compiled the silliest, funniest, most outrageous marks that fans would never find in any other record book. In the following pages, we present the results of our efforts—records of heretofore unknown or little-known ignoble moments from more than a hundred years of baseball, such as:

- Most bonbons eaten by a pitcher before a game
- Most innings played in formal attire

- Most teeth pulled in hopes of pitching better
- Longest time a manager had his foot stuck in a garbage can
- Longest time a player watched an All-Star Game in the nude

Since there's a funny or fascinating story behind these mindless marks, each record is accompanied by a light-hearted anecdote or description of the dubious achievement.

So where did we get all these records? For years, we collected anecdotes from newspaper and magazine clips; team histories; biographies; personal interviews with players, coaches, managers, and umpires; and the archives of the National Baseball Hall of Fame and Museum in Cooperstown, New York. Then we quantified many hilarious happenings into records. Some incidents can't be quantified—like the wackiest finish to a home-run trot or the only pitcher to deliberately throw a wild pitch to lose a game—but nonetheless they deserved recognition and, thus, were included in this book.

Now, don't get on our case if some of the records aren't exact. Sometimes guesstimates were used; other times we relied solely on newspaper accounts. Often we spoke with the record-holder and took his word for the details. In any event, we did our best to document every record. However, we certainly welcome evidence from readers of marks that top the ones we included in this book or of new wacky records that we neglected to compile. Flip to the back of the book to learn how to send your contributions to us. We'd love to hear from you.

Just what does it mean to have one's name etched

in *The Baseball Hall of Shame's Warped Record Book*? It's a true recognition of ignobility. "I always wanted to be in the record books," said former Yankees hurler Jim Bouton, who set the mark for the most times a pitcher's hat fell off in a World Series game (37 times, 1964). "I just never thought it would be because of my cap."

Said former St. Louis Browns pitcher Jim Walkup, "It cost me 50 bucks to make it into your record book—but at least I'm in." In 1935, he established the mark for the stiffest fine ($50) ever given a pitcher for *striking out* a batter.

Just days before Hall of Famer Luke Appling died, he proudly recalled for us the 1940 game when he purposely fouled off a record 24 straight pitches in one at-bat. "I never viewed it as a record at the time," he said, "but, you know, I'm kind of proud of it now."

The grand old game will continue to produce more dubious achievements on and off the field—and we will be there to chronicle them. If it's crazy, funny, or bizarre, you can bet it's one for the record—the *Warped Record Book*, that is.

THE BASEBALL HALL OF SHAME'S
WARPED RECORD BOOK

Bats Incredible!

WARPED RECORDS OF BATTERS

Most pitches fouled off in one at-bat

24 pitches
Luke Appling, Chicago White Sox   1940

No one could deliberately foul off pitches as deftly as Chicago White Sox shortstop and Hall of Famer Luke Appling.

He once fouled off an incredible 24 pitches in one at-bat. It happened in 1940 when the New York Yankees were whipping the Sox, 8–2. "I figured since we weren't going to win anyway, I'd have me a little fun and see if I couldn't wear out [starting pitcher] Red Ruffing," Appling recalled.

"So I started fouling off his pitches. I took a pitch every now and then. Pretty soon, after 24 fouls, old Red could hardly lift his arm and I walked. That's when they took him out of the game and he cussed me all the way to the dugout."

In a game with the Detroit Tigers three years later, Appling pulled off a similar foul feat. Batting against Dizzy Trout, Appling fouled off 14 consecutive pitches. Trout was so ticked off at Appling that on his next pitch, he threw his glove instead of the ball.

Recalled Appling, "I fouled that one off, too."

Most plate appearances in one at-bat

3 appearances
Jeffrey Leonard, Houston Astros   1979

Houston Astros outfielder Jeffrey Leonard made two outs and hit a single . . . during just one at-bat!

On August 21, 1979, the Astros were losing to the New York Mets, 5–0, with two outs in the ninth inning when Leonard came to bat. He flied out to center field, apparently ending the game.

But before the pitch had been thrown, Mets shortstop Frank Taveras had called time out, so the umpires sent Leonard back to the plate.

This time Leonard singled to left field. But when he ran to first base, he found nobody there. Mets first baseman Ed Kranepool had gone to the dugout when the shortstop had called time out.

The umpires ruled that since the Mets didn't have the required nine men on the field, Leonard would have to bat again.

On his third try, Leonard flied out to finally end the game. In a lone at-bat, he'd gone 1-for-3!

Most home runs hit off a laundry building in one game

3 home runs
Roy Campanella, Brooklyn Dodgers   1950

Dodgers catcher Roy Campanella had a spotless day at the plate by blasting three towering homers that all hit a laundry building across the street.

In a 1950 game against the Cincinnati Reds at Crosley Field, Campy reamed, steamed, and dry-cleaned the pitches of Cincy hurler Ken Raffensberger.

In the second inning, Campanella belted a two-run shot that sailed over the left-field wall and landed on the roof of the laundry building more than 400 feet away. Two innings later, Campy socked another two-run homer to the very same spot. Raffensberger walked the Dodgers catcher in the sixth. But in the eighth, Campanella clouted his third two-run round-tripper of the day. The drive soared out of the park and struck the side of the laundry on one bounce.

In leading his team to a 7–5 victory, Campanella had put Raffensberger through the wringer, and hung him out to dry.

Longest time before a pop-up came down

24 hours
Dave Kingman, Oakland Athletics   1984

A's slugger Dave Kingman golfed a pitch against the Minnesota Twins that rocketed high over the infield. The ball soared up, up, and away . . . and didn't come down until the next day!

That's because the ball went through an eight-inch-wide tear in the fabric ceiling of Minneapolis' Metrodome, 180 feet above the pitcher's mound.

All the infielders gazed upward, waiting for the ball to come down. When it didn't, Twins first baseman Micky Hatcher decided to scam the umpires. "I grabbed a ball out of the ump's bag, slammed it against the ground, and tagged Kingman out," said Hatcher. "But they didn't go for it."

Plate umpire Jim Evans ruled the pop-up a ground-rule double. Dome superintendent Dick Davis called Kingman's bizarre pop-up a "million-to-one shot."

The next day, a dome maintenance man crawled up on the roof, poked a stick through a vent, and dislodged the ball—which finally fell to the ground 24 hours after it was hit.

The ball was then sent to the Baseball Hall of Fame in Cooperstown, New York, where it has remained grounded ever since.

Most times hit by a pitch in one at-bat

2 times
Nellie Fox, Chicago White Sox   1956

Nellie Fox had to endure getting bonked by not one but two pitches before the umpire allowed him to take a base.

In a June 3, 1956, game against the Baltimore Orioles, Fox got whacked on the butt by a curveball flung by left-hander Johnny Schmitz. But plate umpire Hank Soar accused Fox of not making an effort to avoid the missile and called the pitch a ball.

Two pitches later, Schmitz hit Fox again. This time the umpire decided Fox had done his best to get out of harm's way and sent the bruised batter limping to first.

Unluckiest batter ever to hit .399

Don Padgett, St. Louis Cardinals   1939

On the final day of the 1939 season, St. Louis Cardinals outfielder Don Padgett needed just one more hit to reach the coveted .400 mark.

But he was a man ahead of his time (out).

Playing against the Chicago Cubs at Wrigley Field, Padgett wanted more than anything to hit .400. Because he had only 233 at-bats, he didn't have enough appearances at the plate to qualify for the batting title. But he did have enough to impress his teammates and the Cardinals' front office.

Sent in as a pinch hitter in the eighth inning, Padgett lined a clean single up the middle. But before he could celebrate, his heart sank. The first base umpire had called time a split second before the pitch was thrown because a ball had rolled loose in the bullpen.

The hit didn't count.

Padgett returned to the plate and drew a walk. That was his last at-bat of the season. Said Cardinals catcher Mickey Owen, "He missed .400 because of that lousy time-out. How unlucky can you get?"

Longest delay of a game while looking for a toothpick

4 minutes
Silent John Titus, Philadelphia Phillies   1905

Silent John Titus, a lifetime .282 hitter, attributed his success at the plate to lucky toothpicks—he always kept one clenched between his teeth when he batted.

"Without my bitin' on that ol' toothpick, I ain't able to hit nothin' past the pitcher," the superstitious slugger once said.

Rival pitchers came to hate the sight of that ever-present toothpick. During a 1905 game, St. Louis Cardinals pitcher Sandy McDougal fired a ball straight at Silent John's mouth, trying to knock the hated toothpick right down his throat. John ducked safely out of the way—but, to his horror, he lost his toothpick.

Frantically, he got down on all fours searching for the sliver, but couldn't find it. After a delay of nearly four minutes, the umpire ordered Silent John to get up and bat. Instead, the batter rushed over to the Phillies dugout and begged his teammates for a toothpick.

But nobody had one. At that point Silent John knew

it was time for Toothpick or Consequences. Like a doomed man, he slowly trudged back to the plate—and struck out.

Worst performance by a player in a game honoring him

Walt Dropo, Detroit Tigers 1953

Detroit first baseman Walt Dropo grew up near Hartford, Connecticut. So when the Tigers played an exhibition game there in 1953, the townspeople honored their local hero by holding a Walt Dropo Day.

The previous season, "Moose," as he was fondly called, had batted .276, clubbed 29 home runs, and batted in 97 runs.

Before the exhibition game, Dropo was showered with praise and gifts, including a new car. But when he took the field, the hero became a zero—he went 0-for-6 at the plate and made three glaring errors at first.

They let him keep the car anyway.

Most times hit into a triple play

4 times
Brooks Robinson, Baltimore Orioles 1959–1973

They called Brooks Robinson "The Vacuum Cleaner" because he sucked up nearly every ball that was hit toward the hot corner. The Hall of Fame third baseman also was a solid hitter. But on four occasions "The Vacuum Cleaner" broke down at the plate.

Robinson holds the dubious distinction of being the only major league player ever to hit into four triple plays.

It's the only one of his many achievements that he'd just as soon forget. After New York Yankees star Graig Nettles broke Robinson's American League career home-run mark for third basemen in 1980, Robinson said wistfully: "I wouldn't mind seeing someone erase my record of hitting into four triple plays."

Longest distance between hits on the same day

785 miles
Joel Youngblood, New York Mets–
Montreal Expos   1982

Joel Youngblood really went to great lengths to get two singles on August 4, 1982. He hit the first one in Chicago . . . and the second one in Philadelphia.

Playing with the New York Mets in Chicago's Wrigley Field that afternoon, the right fielder smacked a third-inning single that scored two runs and helped the Mets win the game.

Just minutes later, Youngblood was told he'd been traded to the Montreal Expos. He promptly caught a plane to Philadelphia, where the Expos were playing that night, and rushed to the ballpark just as the Expos-Phillies game was entering the third inning.

Montreal manager Jim Fanning immediately put Youngblood into the game—and he promptly swatted his second single of the day, 785 miles from the site of the first.

Smallest strike zone in major league history

1½ inches
Eddie Gaedel, St. Louis Browns   1951

Throwing a strike to Browns pinch hitter Eddie Gaedel would have required the accuracy of a laser beam. That's because Eddie was a midget who stood only 3 feet 7 inches tall—and his strike zone when he went into a crouch was a teensy-weensy one and a half inches!

A baseball's diameter is bigger than that.

Wacky Browns owner Bill Veeck sent Eddie up to the plate to pinch-hit during a game with the Detroit Tigers on August 19, 1951. When the little guy made his appearance, wearing number 1/8, the crowd roared with hysterical laughter.

Eddie crouched low with his bat outstretched as pitcher Bob Cain, fighting back giggles, wound up and threw. Eddie let the ball go by. Veeck had told him that if he swung at anything, a rifleman on the roof had orders to shoot him down—and, although it wasn't true, Eddie believed it!

Naturally, Eddie drew a walk on four straight pitches. A pinch runner then was sent in for him, and Eddie retired to the dugout to thunderous applause. It was Eddie's first, and last, appearance in a major league game.

Most consecutive at-bats without a hit after giving up chewing tobacco

8 at-bats
Harvey Kuenn, Detroit Tigers   1958

Slugger Harvey Kuenn was always smokin' at the plate when he had a chaw of tobacco in his mouth. But without that magic wad, he couldn't hit worth a spit.

In 1958, after years of chewing, Kuenn made a bet with the team trainer that he could give up the nasty stuff. But when he tried to bat, Kuenn did just what a rookie does upon trying tobacco for the first time—he choked.

"I went 0-for-8, and I lost the bet," said the Detroit Tigers star. "I went back to chewing." The next year Kuenn never went to the plate without a big chaw in his cheek—and wound up winning the American League batting crown!

Later, as the tobacco-chewing manager of the Milwaukee Brewers, Kuenn led the team to the 1982 World Series. But after the cheering died down, parents in Wauwatosa, Wisconsin, angrily blamed him for a sudden outbreak of tobacco chewing in the town's two high schools.

They said they didn't want their kids becoming spittin' images of the Milwaukee manager.

Most at-bats without ever hitting a ball over the outfield wall

4,164 at-bats
Tommy Thevenow, St. Louis Cardinals–Pittsburgh
Pirates–Philadelphia Phillies–Cincinnati Reds–
Boston Braves   1924–1938

At a spindly 5 feet 10 inches and 155 pounds, infielder Tommy Thevenow looked like the "before" picture in a muscle-building ad.

So it's easy to understand why he established a record for powerless hitting. In 15 years in the majors and 4,164 at-bats, Thevenow never once swatted a ball over the outfield wall!

Tommy had trouble even knocking the ball past the infielders. A lifetime .247 slap hitter, Thevenow averaged fewer than 20 extra-base hits for every 500 at-bats.

There was only one year in his entire career when he experienced the thrill of hitting a home run. In 1926, as a shortstop for the St. Louis Cardinals, Tommy clubbed two round-trippers—both inside-the-parkers. He even swatted an inside-the-park circuit clout during the 1926 World Series when his line drive skipped between New York Yankees left fielder Bob Meusel and center fielder Earle Combs.

But never again in a major league game did Tommy hit a homer. He went homerless the last 12 years of his career. In fact, Thevenow also holds the record for most consecutive at-bats without a homer—3,347.

Loneliest dugout greeting after hitting a home run

Al Rosen, Cleveland Indians   1952

Indians third baseman Al Rosen bounded into the dugout expecting hearty congratulations after blasting a four-bagger at Cleveland's Municipal Stadium. But nobody rushed up to greet him.

Puzzled, he looked toward the other end of the dugout and saw all his teammates huddled around first baseman Luke Easter—who was slumped on the ground like a crumpled bag of balls.

Luke had dozed off on the bench and been jolted awake by the crowd's roar when Rosen hit his homer. "He jumped to his feet and bumped his head on the top of the dugout," recalled Rosen. "He knocked himself out cold."

Biggest salary cut after winning the batting title

$1,000
Frank "Lefty" O'Doul, Brooklyn Dodgers   1932

After Lefty O'Doul led all hitters in the National League with a sizzling .368 average in 1932, the Dodgers' management decided to adjust his salary—they slashed his pay from $9,000 to $8,000.

Not that the Dodgers didn't appreciate his efforts. Poor Lefty just happened to be a man born ahead of his time.

If he'd won the batting title today, the hard-hitting outfielder would have received a huge pay boost and been a millionaire. However, Lefty was playing back in 1932—when the country was in the grip of a growing depression and money was as tight as the webbing of a new glove.

Even with the salary cut, the Dodgers found O'Doul was just too expensive to keep around. Early the next season, O'Doul, who had hit over .300 for five straight years, was traded to the New York Giants.

Most times a player was a 3,000th-strikeout victim

2 times
Cesar Geronimo, Cincinnati Reds   1974, 1980

A mere 10 pitchers in major league history have struck out 3,000 or more batters. And two of the hurlers reached that coveted mark by whiffing the same man!

The ill-fated strikeout victim was Cesar Geronimo, a .258 lifetime hitter and veteran outfielder for the Reds.

On July 17, 1974, he became the 3,000th batter struck out by St. Louis Cardinals fireballer Bob Gibson. Six years later, on July 4, 1980, Geronimo was the luckless guy at the plate when Houston Astros ace Nolan Ryan recorded his 3,000th K.

Most lobsters won for hitting a home run

12 lobsters
Jimmie Foxx, Boston Red Sox   1940

Baseball legend Jimmie Foxx loved seafood almost as much as he loved the game. So when a fan offered him a dozen lobsters if he'd hit a home run, Foxx responded with a game-winning smasheroo!

But until his final at-bat, it appeared the catch of the day was going to get away.

Foxx's Red Sox were playing the Philadelphia Athletics on July 3, 1940. It was a special day for 65-year-old boat captain Israel Baker of Maine, who'd come to Fenway Park to watch the Red Sox—his favorite team for 50 years.

"Before the game I told Jimmie I'd brought a dozen fine lobsters with me," recalled Captain Baker. "I promised him he could have all of them if he hit a homer in that game. If he didn't he'd have to share the lobsters with Ted Williams."

Foxx was determined not to divide the tasty crustaceans with his hard-hitting teammate. But inning after inning went by and Foxx wasn't able to get even a single.

When the Red Sox came up for their final turn at bat, the A's were leading 11–6. With six batters ahead of him, Foxx's chances of getting a home run seemed as dim as a two-watt bulb.

The first batter drew a walk. The second popped out. The next three all hit singles, tallying one run to make the score 11–7. Next up was Ted Williams who smashed a dramatic grand-slam homer that tied the game.

Unbelievably, Foxx got his turn at bat. And when the pitcher tried to slip a curve past him, he slapped it into outer space for a stunning, game-winning round-tripper.

"Jimmie ran right from home plate to me and shook hands," Captain Baker recalled. "I gave him the 12 lobsters, of course—and so far as I know, he ate them all himself."

Longest single ever hit in an indoor stadium

446 feet
Mike Schmidt, Philadelphia Phillies 1974

Mike Schmidt was cheated out of a tape-measure home run at Houston's Astrodome during a 1974 game. His blast sailed high and deep—until it slammed into a loudspeaker hanging from the domed ceiling.

The ball probably would have soared more than 500 feet if Schmidt had been playing in any other ballpark. Instead, it went 329 feet to the speaker and dropped 117 feet down onto center field, travelling 446 feet in all.

Under stadium ground rules, the ball was still in play. Because two base runners had stopped dead as the ball went whizzing high over their heads, Schmidt made it only to first base.

Instead of yet another headline-making home run, the Philadelphia slugger had to settle for the longest indoor single in baseball history.

Most hits in a doubleheader while avoiding a beanball

2 hits
Jiggs Donahue, Chicago White Sox 1906

In one of the wildest freak hitting exhibitions ever, Jiggs Donahue ducked to keep from getting beaned by two high inside pitches—and accidentally wound up with two singles.

Just as amazing, each hit resulted in a run that proved the winning edge in both games of a doubleheader against the St. Louis Browns!

On July 3, 1906, Jiggs got his first weird hit in the third inning of the opener. Browns pitcher Ed Smith threw a fastball that headed straight for the batter's head. As Jiggs whirled away, the ball hit his bat and shot into right field, scoring a runner on second.

The Browns jeered Jiggs for his offbeat batting style the rest of the game. They were still ribbing him when he came to bat in the second game.

Browns hurler Albert "Benny" Jacobson fired a high inside pitch at Jiggs. Again, Jiggs dove out of the way. Again, his bat hit the ball for a line drive single—and again, a runner on second ran home for what turned out to be the winning run!

Only "inside-the-tuba" home run

Willie Stargell, Pittsburgh Pirates 1965

In the 1965 All-Star Game, Willie Stargell tuned up his home-run swing. Literally. In the wackiest four-bagger ever hit in the midseason classic, the Hall of Famer lofted a pitch over the wall—and into a tuba!

It happened in Minnesota's Metropolitan Stadium in the second inning. While facing Twins right-hander Jim "Mudcat" Grant, the Pirates' slugger blasted a fastball that sailed into the right-field bullpen where a band had been playing.

"The ball flew right into the tuba," Stargell recalled with a big belly laugh. "I'm not sure the guy ever got the ball out. I've often wondered."

Most outs made by a batter in 3 trips to the plate

7 outs
Burleigh Grimes, Brooklyn Dodgers   1925

The job of Dodgers hurler Burleigh Grimes was to get outs—but for the other team, not his own.

The batter's box turned into a house of horrors for Grimes during a September 22, 1925, game against the Chicago Cubs. He hit into two double plays, then into a triple killing to rack up a total of seven outs in just three at-bats.

The frustrated hurler got a fourth shot at the plate later in the game. He made another out . . . but at least that time he didn't take anybody back to the bench with him.

When the Dodgers lost, 3–2, Grimes had nobody to blame but himself.

Most times hit by pitches in one day

5 times
Frank Chance, Chicago Cubs   1904

Frank Chance felt like a walking target during a bruising doubleheader. Cincinnati Reds hurlers hit him five times with pitches—one of which nearly killed him.

In the first game, Reds pitcher Jack Harper cut loose with a fastball that sailed high and tight. Chance, the Cubs' captain and first baseman, didn't get out of the way in time. The ball slammed into his face so hard that he was knocked unconscious for several minutes.

"It was a narrow escape, for if the blow had been an inch farther back it would have killed him," said the *Chicago Daily Tribune.*

But iron man Chance struggled to his feet, shook the cobwebs out of his head, and continued to play despite a nasty black eye.

The next time at bat, Harper hit Chance again, this time on the arm, and then plunked him in the side a third time in the game, which the Reds won 7–4.

Though battered and bruised, Chance started the nightcap against Reds hurler Win Kellum. Pitching as though there was a bounty on Chance's head, Kellum nailed him twice with fastballs. But the tough Cub stayed in the game and led his team to a 5–2 victory.

It was obvious that in this doubleheader, the Reds' pitchers seldom missed a Chance.

Longest homer ever hit for an out

450 feet (estimated)
Hank Aaron, Milwaukee Braves   1965

Hammerin' Hank Aaron blasted a monster homer onto the right-field roof of Sportsman's Park in St. Louis, only to be called out—because he had stepped out of the batter's box.

The homer that wasn't occurred in the eighth inning of a 3–3 tie between the Braves and Cardinals, and deprived Aaron of his 28th round-tripper of the season.

When St. Louis hurler Curt Simmons threw a change-up, Aaron was so anxious to hit it, he ran up on the pitch and clubbed it about 450 feet for an apparent homer. But plate umpire Chris Pelekoudas immediately called Aaron out for stepping out of the batter's box.

"Aaron was running up on the change-up," the umpire later explained. "His foot was at least three feet out when he hit the home run."

Milwaukee manager Bobby Bragan immediately challenged the ump and got a quick thumb. "I told Pelekoudas it was either a grudge call or he just wanted to get his name in the papers," said Bragan after the game, which the Braves won 5–3. "That's when he threw me out."

Most batters to strike out in their half of an inning

5 batters
Minnesota Twins   1976

Houston Astros catcher Cliff Johnson was having all sorts of trouble catching the fluttering knuckleball of pitcher Joe Niekro during a 1976 spring training game.

That should have been good news to the Minnesota Twins. But Johnson's failure to hang on to the pitches brought untold embarrassment to the Twins.

That's because Niekro struck out the side—all five batters.

In the top of the first inning, Niekro's knuckler was sensational. The Twins couldn't hit it. Unfortunately for the Astros, Johnson couldn't catch it. He committed five passed balls in the inning, including two on third strikes that allowed both batters to reach first safely. As a result, the Twins kept swinging . . . and missing.

By the time Johnson was able to hang on to a third strike in the inning, five Twins had whiffed.

Shortest "4-bagger" ever hit inside a domed stadium

35 feet
Eric Davis, Cincinnati Reds   1986

Eric Davis tapped a sorry little dribbler that should have been an easy putout. But, incredibly, on that meager hit, he managed to race around the bases and score.

Playing against the Houston Astros in the Astrodome, Davis hit a grounder that lazily rolled 35 feet into the waiting glove of pitcher Nolan Ryan. The hurler fired it to first base, but his throw was wild and the ball bounded into the right-field bullpen for an error.

As Davis rounded second base, right fielder Kevin Bass picked up the ball and threw it to third. But his throw also was wild for the second error—and Davis romped home.

Said amazed Reds manager Pete Rose: "I haven't seen anything like that since Little League."

Wackiest finish to a home-run trot

Sammy White, Boston Red Sox   1952

The Red Sox were losing to the St. Louis Browns, 9–7, in the bottom of the ninth inning when Boston catcher Sammy White walloped a grand slam to win the game.

Thrilled beyond belief, White proudly trotted around

the bases as the Fenway Park faithful cheered their lungs out. Then White capped off his four-bagger with a flourish.

About 10 feet from home, he dropped to his hands and knees and slowly crept up to the plate. And when he finally got there, the crazy catcher leaned over and kissed home!

Most bases reached by a batter on a foul ball

3 bases
Jake Jones, Boston Red Sox   1947

Even though Boston batter Jake Jones swatted a foul ball that rolled only 60 feet, he ended up safe at third because of an obscure rule.

Jones's unique hit came with two outs and the bases empty in the sixth inning of a game against the St. Louis Browns on July 27, 1947. The ball lazily rolled outside the third base line, an obvious foul. But Browns pitcher Fred Sanford feared it might veer back into fair territory for an infield hit. So the hurler threw his glove at the ball, hit it and kept it foul.

According to the rules at the time, a batter was awarded a triple if a fielder threw his glove at a batted ball. In 1954, the rule was amended to apply only to fair balls. That was seven years too late for the Browns.

As soon as Sanford's glove touched the ball, umpire Cal Hubbard awarded Jones a triple. Jones later scored and the Red Sox went on to win, 4–3.

Most bets won by a batter on one hit

51 bets
Bob "Fat" Fothergill, Chicago White Sox   1930

When high-spirited slugger Bob "Fat" Fothergill learned he'd been sold by the Detroit Tigers to the Chicago White Sox, he made 51 separate bets with friends that he would hit safely in his first at-bat with his new team.

A few days after "Fat" waddled out of Detroit, all 51 of his pals received identical telegrams saying: "PAY UP. I SINGLED TO LEFT."

Most bases reached by a batter after hitting a frog

3 bases
Roy Johnson, Detroit Tigers   1931

In a game against the Cleveland Indians, Detroit's Roy Johnson whacked a line drive that bounced on the ground just beyond second base for what looked like a routine single.

But then a frog hopped into the picture.

The fat amphibian had been snoozing in the high outfield grass when center fielder Earl Averill's approaching footsteps woke him up. Frightened, the toad jumped high into the air—and smacked into the ball at the top of his leap.

The collision sent the ball bounding away from Averill's glove. By the time the startled outfielder recovered and chased down the ball, lucky Johnson was safe on third.

Mr. Frog, however, wasn't safe. He croaked.

Most wind-blown home runs in one game

7 homers
Philadelphia Phillies vs. Chicago Cubs   1979

In a rock 'em, sock 'em game between the Cubs and the visiting Phillies, 11 homers were walloped—including seven that were gone with the (Wrigley Field) wind.

With a strong, steady, 20-mile-per-hour breeze—and gusts up to 30 miles per hour—blowing out, batters licked their chops and tried to sock balls up into the jet stream and out of the ballpark. Before the game, veteran Philadelphia left fielder Del Unser estimated that the Windy City wind would power the ball at least an extra 80 feet. It didn't take long to prove him right.

In the top of the first inning, Mike Schmidt, Bob Boone, and Randy Lerch all lofted balls that the wind carried over the wall for homers. Later, Mother Nature gave an assist to a Garry Maddox round-tripper as the Phils soared to a 17–6 lead over Chicago—and it was still only the top of the fourth inning!

But then, the Cubs set sail in the stiff breeze. Steve Ontiveros and Jerry Martin hit the fifth and sixth wind-blown homers of the game. Bill Buckner clubbed the seventh, only his was a grand slam. Meanwhile, slugger Dave Kingman blasted three round-trippers, but none of them needed any help from the wind.

"We were a little worried out in the bullpen," said

Phils relief ace Tug McGraw. "We knew that on a day like this, the pitcher was going to get the crap kicked out of him." McGraw found out for himself. He gave up seven runs (and two homers) in two-thirds of an inning.

Incredibly, the Cubs, who in the fifth inning trailed the Phils by as much as 21–9, stormed back to tie the score at 22–22 in the eighth. But Schmidt broke the deadlock in the tenth with a game-winning monster homer that would have left the park even without the wind.

Said Philadelphia shortstop Larry Bowa, "Nowhere else in the world would there be a ball game like this except on a windy day at Wrigley Field."

Most years in the majors before getting his first triple

10½ years
Harry Spilman, San Francisco Giants   1988

Utility man Harry Spilman somehow managed to make it into his 11th season in the bigs without hitting a triple—an impotent batting record unequalled by any other nonpitcher.

Not until his 506th career game and 749th at-bat did he finally smack a three-bagger. And it happened against a pitcher who was really an infielder!

On June 28, 1988, the San Francisco Giants were blowing out the Atlanta Braves, so Braves third baseman Jim Morrison came in to pitch. He served up a slow fastball that Spilman hit into the power alley.

Asked when he knew he had the triple, Spilman replied, "When I was standing on the bag."

The jubilation over Harry's feat was felt "not only in our clubhouse but the whole baseball world," said teammate Bob Brenley. "You could almost sense that the Braves wanted to come across the field and congratulate him, too."

The Braves should've known Spilman was a dangerous man. After all, only 14 months earlier, he'd stolen his first base—after more than nine years in the majors.

"Harry's hot," said his proud manager, Roger Craig. "He's got a stolen base and a triple in back-to-back seasons."

Most poisonous snakes clubbed to death with a bat

8 snakes
Luis Vasquez, Cincinnati Reds   1990

The Reds had plenty of runs, hits, and terrors during spring training after discovering that a pond adjoining their Plant City, Florida, camp was crawling with venomous water moccasins!

As his terrified teammates warily watched where they stepped during practice, pitcher Luis Vasquez went on the offensive and clubbed eight of the uninvited baseball fangs to death with a bat.

Relief pitcher Randy Myers captured another deadly serpent with a squeegie and carried it into the clubhouse—scaring the wits out of his fellow players.

For the rest of training camp, Vasquez and his teammates walked softly and carried a big stick.

A Farewell to Arms
WARPED RECORDS OF PITCHERS

Most teeth pulled in hopes of pitching better

4 teeth
Lee "Lefty" Grissom, Cincinnati Reds   1938

Pitching with a chronically sore arm in 1938, south-paw Lefty Grissom eagerly listened up when someone told him that hurler Lefty Grove, by then destined for the Hall of Fame, once had two teeth pulled to restore his throwing arm.

That's the secret to getting my arm back in shape! thought Grissom. He rushed to a dentist and had two teeth extracted—then two more for good measure. He never stopped to wonder how yanking four good teeth had any bearing on his pitching arm. Until later.

"I think somebody was filling me full of it," Grissom ruefully recalled years later. "But it seemed like a good idea when I heard about it. I figured if I could win some games, it was worth it.

"The teeth-pulling didn't hurt me. I was back to pitching in a couple of days. But it damn sure didn't help my arm none!"

Lefty's record that ruthless, toothless season: two wins, three losses, and one bill for false choppers.

Most batters faced in a career without getting anyone out

7 batters
Elmer "Doc" Hamann, Cleveland Indians   1922

Rookie reliever Elmer Hamann was so nervous when he was thrust into his first and only major league game that he never got a single batter out.

With the Cleveland Indians trailing the visiting Boston Red Sox, 9–5, on September 21, 1922, Hamann entered the game in the ninth inning—and couldn't find the strike zone with a road map.

Shaking like a leaf, the scared 22-year-old walked the first two batters he faced, Johnny Mitchell and Ed Chaplin. Then he accidentally beaned the next batter, opposing pitcher Jack Quinn, to load the bases.

Hamann was more frazzled than ever and walked Mike Menosky, forcing in a run. The hurler finally got the ball over the plate—only to watch Elmer Miller blast it for a bases-clearing triple. The rattled rookie then gave up a run-scoring single to George Burns, uncorked a wild pitch, and yielded another RBI base hit to Del Pratt, which now made the score 15–5.

Manager Tris Speaker had seen enough. He mercifully yanked Hamann, who never again played in a major league game.

The statistics for Hamann's entire career of facing seven batters: three hits, three walks, six runs, one wild pitch, one hit batsman . . . and no outs.

Most weight put on by a pitcher during the off-season

68 pounds
Walter "Jumbo" Brown, Cleveland Indians
1927–1928

Pitcher Walter Brown weighed 197 pounds at the end of the 1927 season. But when he waddled into spring training camp only a few months later, he crunched the scale at 265!

For some mysterious reason, Brown began ballooning after having his tonsils removed during the off-season. And after spring training he continued to pack on the flab until he wound up the heaviest player in modern baseball history—a 295-pound behemoth who was aptly nicknamed "Jumbo."

Despite working out for hours a day, he simply couldn't shed the weight. Quipped one sportswriter: "He throws a fastball, a curve, and the biggest shadow in baseball." Said another: "He weighs two pounds more than an elephant, but that's an exaggeration—by two pounds, anyway."

Jumbo pitched in only five games for Cleveland in 1928 and ended up with an 0–1 record and a hefty 6.75 ERA. The Indians then sent him back to the minors where, one scribe wrote, "Jumbo hopefully can pitch more and eat less."

Most runs given up in a no-hitter that was lost

4 runs
Andy Hawkins, New York Yankees   1990

Every pitcher dreams of throwing a no-hitter, but Andy Hawkins had nightmares after achieving the feat—because he lost the game, 4–0.

No other major league pitcher has ever tossed a nine-inning complete game no-hitter and wound up on the wrong side of such a lopsided score.

Hawkins, who three weeks earlier was dangerously close to being cut by the Yankees, was hurling a phenomenal game against the Chicago White Sox on July 1, 1990. He was cutting down batters like Paul Bunyan set loose on a stand of saplings.

For seven innings, Handy Andy's luck held. Then in the bottom of the eighth, the Yankees committed three errors, including two dropped fly balls, and gifted the Sox with four unearned runs.

"I was stunned," the unhappy hurler said as he stood shaking his head in disbelief after the game. "This is not even close to the way I envisioned a no-hitter would be."

Fastest collapse of a pitcher who pigged out before a game

1 warm-up pitch
Fred Toney, New York Giants   1919

Fred Toney was a terror at the plate—the dinner plate, that is. When food of any kind was put in front of him, the 6-foot-6-inch, 250-pound hurler turned into a human garbage disposal.

Due to start a game in St. Louis one day in 1919, the hefty pitcher started the morning by wolfing down a gigantic breakfast of eggs, toast, bacon, fruit, and a big steak. En route to the park, he got hungry again and gobbled down several hot dogs, nearly a carton of soda, and several pints of ice cream.

At the clubhouse Toney was still famished, so he chowed down on some more hot dogs.

Then the porky pitcher waddled out to the mound, let out a loud BUURRRPPP, threw one warm-up pitch—and collapsed in a heap.

Most bonbons eaten by a pitcher before a game

24 bonbons
Ed Reulbach, Chicago Cubs   1908

Big Ed Reulbach pitched one of the biggest games of his career while loaded to the gills—with sugar.

The Cubs were in a tight pennant race when, an hour before an important contest, Reulbach was hit by a sudden craving for sweets. So he sent the batboy out for a box of 24 chocolate bonbons and began madly stuffing them into his mouth.

Teammates watched Big Ed's eating orgy in horror. Just three months earlier, lightweight boxing champ Joe Gans had lost his title after gorging on candy just before a match.

"Are you crazy?" second baseman Johnny Evers shrieked at Reulbach. "Don't you know what happened to Joe Gans?"

But the pitcher kept pigging out until he had polished off the whole box.

Then Reulbach proved that, as a pitching aid, candy is dandy. He went out and threw a two-hitter!

Most runs allowed by a pitcher while arguing a call

2 runs
David Cone, New York Mets   1990

Pitcher David Cone was so caught up in a squabble with an umpire that he didn't hear his own teammates' warning screams that runners were scoring at will behind his back.

Cone's boneheaded blunder came in a game against the Atlanta Braves on April 30, 1990. As first baseman Mike Marshall chased after a grounder, Cone raced to cover first. Second baseman Gregg Jefferies fielded the ball and flipped it to Cone for what the pitcher thought was the inning-ending out.

But umpire Charlie Williams called the runner safe, telling Cone he hadn't touched the base. Cone exploded and began loudly protesting the call.

Braves runner Dale Murphy, who was on third, noticed Cone's back was to him and began sneaking down the line—then broke for home. Other Mets saw the steal and hollered at Cone to no avail.

"I was yelling as loud as I could at Dave," said Jefferies. Meanwhile, Braves runner Ernie Whitt had gone from second to third and was eyeing Cone. He, too, bolted for home—while Jefferies frantically grabbed Cone and tried to turn him around!

But the pitcher was oblivious to everything but umpire Williams—until the ump mockingly told him: "While you're arguing, another run just scored."

Cone finally came back down to earth. But his Mets never recovered from his pair of freebies and lost, 7–4.

The pitcher lamely explained: "I just snapped."

Said miffed Mets manager Dave Johnson: "I've seen some strange things in my life in baseball, but this is up there on top of the list."

Only pitcher to deliberately throw a wild pitch to lose a game

Jack Nabors, Philadelphia Athletics 1916

On his way to a record 19 straight defeats in 1916, hard-luck pitcher Jack Nabors became resigned to losing.

Although he pitched his heart out and recorded a decent 3.47 ERA in over 200 innings, he won only one game and lost 20 with the last-place A's—a weak-hitting club that won only 36 games all year.

Nabors's frustration was never more evident than during the no-hitter he was pitching against the Boston

Red Sox. Holding on to a 1–0 lead, Nabors got the first out in the ninth inning before walking the next batter.

Whitey Witt then booted a potential game-ending double-play grounder, putting runners on first and second. A moment later, the heartsick Nabors lost his no-hitter on a single to center.

But there was still hope of victory. Center fielder Wally Schang scooped up the ball and fired home to head off the run. The throw was perfect. But catcher Billy Meyer got tangled up in his own feet and the ball caromed off the heel of his glove as the runner scored the tying tally. The other runners moved up an extra base on the play at the plate and now were perched on second and third with one out.

Nabors surveyed the situation. He looked at the runner on third, took a deep breath ... and deliberately hurled the next pitch high off the backstop, allowing the winning run to trot across the plate.

"What did you do that for?" Meyer asked Nabors.

"Listen," the weary pitcher said grimly. "I knew we'd never get another run. If you think I'm gonna pitch eight more hitless innings in this hot sun, you're nuts."

Most expensive plate of ribs eaten by a relief pitcher during a game

$250
Charlie Kerfeld, Houston Astros   1987

Chubby Charlie Kerfeld was dieting in a desperate effort to lose some of his 248 pounds when, during a July 1987 game in New York, he experienced every dieter's nightmare.

As the Astros' hurler sat in the Shea Stadium bullpen, he smelled the appetizing aroma of barbecued ribs coming from a charity picnic being tossed right behind the bullpen.

Charlie's willpower melted. He sneaked some cash through a bullpen gate to buy a plate of ribs, then skulked off into a corner where he demolished them with gusto.

Unfortunately for Charlie, a TV camera caught him in the act of chomping away. The viewing audience included Astros officials, who promptly fined the pork-loving pitcher $250 for violating a ban on food in the bullpen.

"That definitely was the most expensive plate of ribs I've ever eaten," admitted Kerfeld. "But, boy, were they good."

Most consecutive walks issued by a pitcher in one inning

7 walks
Dolly Gray, Washington Senators   1909

Pitcher Dolly Gray got writer's cramp from scribbling free passes to first base in a 1909 game against the Chicago White Sox. He walked a record seven straight batters—all in the second inning.

After a leadoff single and a sacrifice, the parade of walks began. Sox batters barely had time to say "Hello, Dolly" before he sent them strolling to first.

Said the *Washington Star*: "It looked like a military drill. Each batsman went to the plate and stayed just long enough to permit Gray to write out his pass and then sedately marched to first, while someone would just as sedately walk in from third. It's a fact that the players sat on the bags waiting for the next man to push them along."

After Gray had issued his sixth straight walk, forcing in the fourth run of the inning, Senators second baseman Germany Schaefer offered to change positions with him, but manager Joe Cantillon wouldn't let them.

Gray then gave up his seventh consecutive base on balls, allowing the fifth run to score. When the next batter, Patsy Dougherty, headed for the plate, according to the *Star*, Sox manager Billy Sullivan "did not want him to take a club, but Pat insisted and grounded out." That finally ended the string of walks, although another run scored. Gray then loaded the bases again with a walk but got out of further trouble on a groundout.

For the record, Gray gave up six runs on eight walks and one hit in the inning. He pitched the entire game, shutting out the Sox the rest of the way and walking only three more batters. But that one inning of uncontrollable misery did him in. Gray lost, 6–4.

Most consecutive homers given up at the start of a game

3 homers
Roger Mason, San Francisco Giants   1987

Hurler Roger Mason tried his whole bag of tricks at the start of a game against the San Diego Padres—and watched his pitching skills disappear.

First, Mason tried to slip a slider past Marvell Wynne. But Wynne hammered it for a home run. Next, the pitcher tried a fastball against Tony Gwynn. But Gwynn whacked it out for another round-tripper.

Finally, Mason threw a split-fingered fastball to John Kruk. That, too, went for a four-bagger.

It was the first time in major league history that the first three batters up hit homers. After the cloutburst, Mason moaned: "I'm glad I didn't have a fourth pitch."

Most grand slams served up in one inning

2 grand slams
Silver Bill Phillips, Pittsburgh Pirates   1890

The Pirates felt like making pitcher Silver Bill Phillips walk the plank after he let the Chicago Cubs score eight runs in one inning . . . on two bad pitches.

A century after that fiasco, Phillips remains the only big-league pitcher ever to allow two grand slams in one inning.

Silver Bill served the Cubs two gopher balls, both coming with the bases loaded in the fifth inning of an 1890 game. Chicago third baseman Tom Burns walloped the first grand slam off Phillips, and moments later catcher Malachi Kittridge followed suit. Silver Bill was finally yanked as Chicago coasted to an easy 18–5 victory.

Because his teammates kept reminding him not to throw home-run balls, the hurler gained a new nickname—Whoa Bill.

Most times a pitcher's hat fell off in a World Series game

37 times
Jim Bouton, New York Yankees 1964

It was really hats off for pitcher Jim Bouton, who won Game 3 of the 1964 World Series—he threw so hard, his cap kept flying off his noggin!

Bouton won the game, 2–1 . . . and lost his hat 37 times.

"My cap used to come off all the time when I pitched, because of my motion. But no one had ever kept track of how many times it came off in a game before," he said.

"It was just that it was a World Series game, and in that atmosphere they keep track of everything that happens. So someone started counting. By the end of the game, the radio and television announcers kept saying, 'There goes Bouton's hat again.' "

Most runs given up in an inning on wild pitches

3 runs
Phil Niekro, Atlanta Braves 1979

In a 1979 game against the Houston Astros, Braves pitcher Phil Niekro was throwing wicked knuckleballs. Unfortunately, they were too wicked for his own good.

Niekro set a National League record by throwing four wild pitches in an inning—three of which allowed Astro runners to score from third base.

Trying to protect a 2–0 lead in the bottom of the fifth inning, Niekro gave up a leadoff double to Jose Cruz. After a pop-up and a wild pitch, Niekro walked Jeffrey Leonard. After another pop-up, the hurler struck out Bruce Bochy—but on a wild pitch. As a result, Cruz scored from third and Bochy reached first safely.

Jimmy Sexton then struck out on a dipping knuckleball that got by catcher Bruce Benedict, who then threw to first baseman Dale Murphy. But Murphy dropped the ball for an error. That loaded the bases with two outs.

Niekro then uncorked his third and fourth wild pitches of the inning, allowing Leonard and Bochy to score the second and third runs of the frame—all on errant pitches.

Niekro, who lost the game, 6–2, moaned, "My knuckleball worked too well."

Longest time between pitches by a hurler in one game

5 hours, 9 minutes
Steve Carlton, Philadelphia Phillies   1980

Phillies ace Steve Carlton had a no-hitter going against San Francisco until Mother Nature stepped up to the plate and slammed the stadium with a cloudburst that forced Carlton to cool his heels in the dugout for more than five hours.

The Phils had just come to bat in the bottom of the fourth inning when a rainstorm delayed the game for 1 hour, 28 minutes. Moments later, a second storm hit and shut down the action for another 3 hours, 32 minutes—one of the longest single rain delays ever.

When Carlton finally got back on the mound at the start of the fifth inning, 5 hours and 9 minutes had elapsed since his last pitch in the fourth.

It was an all-time record for time between pitches by a hurler in one game—and the long layoff wrecked Carlton's chances for a no-hitter. The Giants rained on his parade with a 3–1 victory that ended at 3:11 A.M. with only 200 of the original 28,702 fans still on hand.

Most no-hitters blown by a pitcher due to his slow running

3 no-hitters
Spittin' Bill Doak, St. Louis Cardinals   1920, 1922

The slow feet of Spittin' Bill Doak cost him three no-hitters.

Doak lost his first chance in a 1920 game against the Philadelphia Phillies. On a grounder to the first baseman, Doak ran to cover first. But he moved with the speed of a sloth on Sominex and the batter beat him to the bag. It was Philadelphia's only hit of the game.

Two years later, Dave Bancroft of the New York Giants laid down a bunt toward the mound. But slowpoke Doak couldn't get to the ball in time to throw Bancroft out. The Giants said hello to their only hit of the contest, and Doak bid adieu to his second chance at a no-hitter.

Just two months later, fate gave the pitcher a third opportunity for a no-no. Philadelphia batter Curt Walker hit a roller to the first baseman. Doak headed for first to cover the base, but again lost the race. It was the Phils' only hit of the day—and the last chance Doak ever got for baseball immortality.

Most pitchers who failed to get the same batter out in a game

6 pitchers
Chicago Cubs 1964

The Chicago Cubs wore a path to the bullpen trying to retire San Francisco Giants batter Jesus "Jay" Alou. Six Chicago hurlers faced him in a 1964 game—and he smacked a hit off every one of them.

Alou singled off starting pitcher Dick Ellsworth in the first inning, singled off Lew Burdette in the third, singled off Don Elston in the fourth, homered off Dick Scott in the sixth, singled off Wayne Schurr in the seventh, and singled off Lindy McDaniel in the ninth.

Thanks to the Cubs' inability to silence Alou's bat, the Giants easily won the game, 10–3. With a touch of sarcasm in his voice, Chicago third sacker Ron Santo said after the game, "I bet Jay wishes we had sent a seventh pitcher out there."

Most embarrassing finish to a pitcher's career

Bill Fischer, Minnesota Twins 1964

The final pitch in the major league career of Minnesota Twins fireballer Bill Fischer was belted for a home run that cost him the game.

With the score tied, 5–5, in the bottom of the ninth, Baltimore Orioles batter John Orsino had a 3-and-1 count with two out. The Twins then called in Fischer, who'd set a major league record two years earlier by pitching 84⅓ innings without giving up a base on balls.

Fischer strode confidently out to the mound. He stretched, looked, and fired. "Stee-RIKE!" yelled the umpire.

Fischer smiled. Piece of cake. He wound up and threw again.

Orsino nailed the ball dead-solid perfect and sent it whizzing over the fence for a game-winning home run—and Fischer went home a loser in his very last major league game.

Biggest pay raise after losing 19 games

$650,000
Tim Leary, New York Yankees   1990

On the pitching mound, Tim Leary couldn't win for losing in 1990, chalking up a miserable 9–19 record and a woeful 4.11 ERA.

But in his pocketbook, Leary actually won for losing.

Despite his embarrassing stats, the Yankees boosted Leary's salary a whopping $650,000 from $825,000 to $1.475 million for 1991. And that doesn't include the $1 million bonus for signing a three-year contract that calls for salaries of $1.675 million in 1992 and $1.8 million in 1993!

In other words, the front office rewarded Leary with a raise of $34,210.53 for every one of his losses!

The Yankees were kind to Leary in one other way.

Manager Stump Merrill elected not to use Leary the last two weeks of the 1990 season so that the hurler would not run the risk of losing 20 games—a pitcher's most embarrassing statistic.

Worst loss suffered by a hurler who pitched to only one batter

21–2
Wayne LaMaster, Philadelphia Phillies 1938

When the Chicago Cubs clobbered the Philadelphia Phillies, 21–2, the hurler least responsible for the rout was Wayne LaMaster—the losing pitcher.

All he did was face one batter—the Cubs' leadoff hitter, Stan Hack. With the count 1-and-1, LaMaster fired a ball high and away and felt a sharp pain in his throwing arm. He was too hurt to continue, so Phils manager Jimmie Wilson brought in reliever Tommy Reis, who then walked Hack. According to the scoring rules, the walk was charged to LaMaster.

Hack eventually scored one of four Chicago runs in the inning, and the Cubs pounded Philadelphia pitchers for 21 runs and 18 hits. LaMaster had the misfortune of being the pitcher of record because he was responsible for the first runner to score. Since the Phils never came close to tying the game, LaMaster was tagged with the loss in the slaughter—even though he made only three pitches to one batter.

Longest time trapped in bathroom during a game

15 minutes
Bob McClure, Milwaukee Brewers   1979

When teammates locked him in the bullpen bathroom on a hot summer day, relief pitcher Bob McClure had to sweat it out for 15 steaming-hot minutes.

Sweating and screaming, cursing and kicking, McClure demanded to be set free. But his fellow hurlers didn't take him out of the outhouse oven until he was well done.

"I swear it was 115 degrees inside, like a hot box," McClure recalled.

He had entered the bathroom unaware he was about to be the victim of a prank. The flagpole at Milwaukee County Stadium was directly above the bathroom, and the pole's cord hung just above the door. As McClure worked relief inside, his teammates pulled the cord down and wrapped it around the doorknob.

When McClure tried to leave, the door wouldn't budge. He pushed frantically, but he still couldn't get it open.

"I was in there for 15 minutes, yanking so hard on the door the flagpole almost bent in half," he said. "It looked like I had a big old bass on the end of that pole."

Most managers that a hurler pitched for in one season

7 managers
Dock Ellis, New York Yankees–Oakland Athletics–
Texas Rangers   1977

Pitcher Dock Ellis toiled for more major league managers in one year than any player in baseball history —a magnificent *seven*!

Dock started the 1977 season in Yankee pinstripes, toiling for Billy Martin (1). But after pitching in three games in April, Ellis was traded to the Athletics, for whom he appeared in only seven games. In June, a week after Jack McKeon (2) was fired as the A's manager and replaced by Bobby Winkles (3), Dock was sold to the Rangers.

It was just his luck to join a team in turmoil. A week after Dock's arrival, Texas began replacing one manager after another. As a Ranger that year, Ellis played under four skippers—Frank Lucchesi (4), Eddie Stanky (5), Connie Ryan (6), and Billy Hunter (7).

Strangest reward for pitching a shutout

1 chicken
Earl Caldwell, Chicago White Sox   1945

The White Sox and Detroit Tigers were playing a ho-hum game when suddenly, in the fourth inning, a bleacher fan tossed a red hen onto the outfield grass at Comiskey Park.

Detroit center fielder Roger Cramer chased down the

bird and found a note tied to its neck that said: "This chicken is a present for the pitcher who wins the game." Cramer then trotted to the Detroit bench and handed the foul fowl to the Tigers' trainer to hold in escrow until the end of the game.

Egged on by the chance to win the walking meal, White Sox pitcher Earl Caldwell pitched a 5–0 shutout—and invited the dumb cluck home for dinner.

Most losses in a season after being sent down to the minors

31 losses
Ike Butler, Portland Beavers   1903

Ike Butler looked like a promising pitcher when he joined the Baltimore Orioles in 1902. But they didn't like Ike after he ended the season with 10 losses and just one win—and a whopping ERA of 5.34.

Sent back to the minors after just one season, Ike decided to hone his craft with the minor-league Portland Beavers. Instead, he set a Pacific Coast League record by losing an astounding 31 games in 1903.

The only thing Ike didn't lose that year was his confidence. Undismayed, he returned to Portland for the next season . . . and lost 31 games again!

Most consecutive starts at the beginning of a career without having a run scored for him

4 starts
Jim McAndrew, New York Mets   1968

Jim McAndrew should have sued his teammates for nonsupport.

In his first four major league starts for the Mets, McAndrew had an ERA of 1.87—yet he lost all four games because New York failed to score a single run.

He gave up one run in six innings in his major league debut in the Mets' 2–0 loss to the St. Louis Cardinals. In his next start, McAndrew was touched for two runs in 4⅔ innings and lost to the Los Angeles Dodgers, 2–0. Against the San Francisco Giants, the rookie right-hander gave up a lone run in seven innings only to come out a 1–0 loser. The exact same thing happened in his fourth start—one run in seven innings—in a 1–0 loss to the Houston Astros.

When the Mets finally broke their scoreless streak by tallying two runs in the third inning of his next start, the experience so unnerved McAndrew that he was racked for six runs in 4⅔ innings in a 13–3 rout by the Giants.

Finally, McAndrew realized that if he wanted to win a game for the Mets, he had better pitch a shutout. He proceeded to blank the Cardinals in a complete-game five-hitter. But it was no easy victory. The Mets made him wait until the eighth inning before scoring their only run of the game.

The latest gopher ball ever thrown

3:32 A.M.
Tom Gorman, New York Mets   1985

The New York Mets beat the Atlanta Braves, 16–13, in a 19-inning marathon that ended in Atlanta-Fulton County Stadium at 3:55 A.M., on July 5, 1985.

It was the latest ending of any night game in major league history. It would have been over hours earlier if Mets hurler Tom Gorman hadn't given up a game-tying, two-out, two-strike homer—twice.

After rain delays of 84 and 41 minutes, the Mets and Braves went into extra innings tied at 8–8. In the top of the 13th, the Mets scored two runs and then Gorman came on to protect the lead at about 1:30 A.M.. He was one pitch away from picking up the save. But with a runner on first and two out, Terry Harper clubbed Gorman's 0-and-2 fastball off the left-field foul pole, tying the game at 10–10.

For the weary fans and the dog-tired players, sleep would have to wait.

The game remained deadlocked until the 18th inning when the Mets pushed across another run. Gorman then easily got the first two outs. Up to the plate stepped Rick Camp, a pitcher who had only 10 hits and no homers in 165 previous career at-bats. Gorman threw two quick strikes. He was one pitch away from a win . . . and some sleep.

But as the clock showed 3:32 A.M., Gorman grooved another fastball that the weak-hitting Camp socked over the left-field wall for an incredible game-tying home run.

The Mets finally won it with five runs in the top of

the 19th and Ron Darling closed it out in the bottom of the frame after giving up two unearned runs.

Said Gorman after the Mets' 16–13 win, "To give up a homer to the pitcher in the 18th is totally embarrassing. But I never pitched at 3:30 in the morning."

Silliest excuse for leaving a game

Zane Smith, Atlanta Braves   1988

In a July 19, 1988, game against the Philadelphia Phillies, Braves Pitcher Zane Smith suddenly benched himself in the second inning—claiming that his right foot had fallen asleep!

Longest belch by a pitcher

10 seconds
Larry Andersen, Boston Red Sox   1990

Relief hurler Larry Andersen brought a breath of fresh air to the Red Sox clubhouse with a record burp.

His teammates were gloomy and disconsolate in the locker room after dropping their third straight game to the Oakland A's.

Then Andersen walked in with a beer in his hand. He plunked himself down on a storage trunk, took a long swig of beer, reared back his head, and then let out an ear-splitting "BURRRRRRPPPPPP!"

Andersen's world-class belch went on for an amazing 10 solid seconds that left everyone in the clubhouse frozen in fascination. When the belch ended, Andersen noticed all eyes on him. "Lighten up, boys!" he boomed.

As the Burper King ambled toward the showers, his hushed teammates erupted in laughter. The gloom was lifted—and the Red Sox won their next two games.

Most balls called on a pitcher before a batter ever stepped into the box

3 balls
John Boozer, Philadelphia Phillies 1968

Bud Harrelson of the New York Mets became the first batter in history to step into the box with a 3-and-0 count—thanks to spit and stubbornness.

The Mets were beating the Philadelphia Phillies, 3–0, in a 1968 game as Phils reliever John Boozer took the mound in the seventh inning. When plate umpire Ed Vargo saw Boozer spit on his hands before his first warm-up throw, the ump decided the pitcher had violated the league's spitball rule.

"Ball one!" yelled Vargo.

Astounded Phillies manager Gene Mauch roared out of the dugout, screaming, "Ball one? How can it be ball one? He's only warming up!"

"Makes no difference," countered Vargo. "As long as he's on the pitching mound, he can't wet his hand."

"What if I tell him to go to his mouth again?" Mauch angrily asked.

"Then it will be ball two," Vargo snapped.

Mauch ordered Boozer to wet his fingers again—and the umpire yelled, "Ball two!"

Mad enough to spit, Mauch roared, "What if I tell him to go to his mouth *again*?"

"Then it'll be ball three—and he's going to get thrown out of the game!" Vargo snapped.

Mauch ordered Boozer to do it again. The umpire followed through on his threat—and ejected both the pitcher and the manager.

The Phils then brought in reliever Dick Hall to face Harrelson, who was leading off the inning with a comfortable 3-and-0 count. But Harrelson failed to take advantage of the situation. He took two quick strikes before grounding out.

The next day, National League President Warren Giles admitted Vargo was wrong and that the spitball rule didn't apply during warm-up tosses.

Said Mauch, "I've seen managers overmanage, but this is the first time I've ever seen an umpire over-umpire."

Fewest curveballs tossed by a pitcher who told the opposing team he wouldn't throw any

0 curve balls
Dizzy Dean, St. Louis Cardinals   1934

Whatever else he might have been, flamboyant pitcher Dizzy Dean was a man of his word.

Shortly before a game against the Boston Braves in 1934, the future Hall of Famer loudly announced to the opposing players and everyone else within hearing distance that he wasn't going to toss a curveball the whole game.

"I ain't throwin' nothin' but fastballs," Dean declared.

Sure enough, he didn't bend a ball all afternoon. And

51

ol' Diz still shut out the Braves, 3–0—giving up only three hits the whole game.

Heaviest pitcher to ever appear on "Letterman"

270 pounds
Terry Forster, Atlanta Braves   1985

After watching the Braves' 270-pound reliever Terry Forster pitch in a game, late-night TV talk-show host David Letterman branded the portly pitcher a "fat tub of goo" and cracked that he "eats anything that isn't nailed down."

Did Forster sue? Fat chance! Instead, he agreed to appear on Letterman's show. Before the beer-bellied hurler waddled onto the stage, Letterman announced that he'd taken the precaution of having it reinforced. Forster countered by divulging that his personal ambition was to lower his ERA to Letterman's IQ— "0.98."

Forster came on the show in a jacket carrying two cans of Coke, three bags of M&M's, a Nestle Crunch, an Almond Joy, a package of Nibs, seven hot dogs, and a triple-decker David Letterman Sandwich from the Stage Delicatessen that Forster said featured "lots of tongue."

Forster told Letterman that he hadn't always been that big. "It just sort of snacked up on me," he confessed.

The well-rounded pitcher soon met with lean times back in Atlanta, where the Braves released him at the end of the season.

Most home runs given up by one pitcher to Babe Ruth

17 homers
Rube Walberg, Philadelphia Athletics–Boston
Red Sox   1923–1934

Former lumberjack and trapper Rube Walberg was like a babe in the woods when it came to putting down Babe Ruth. Walberg was tagged for 17 homers by the Bambino—more than the Sultan of Swat slugged off any other big league hurler.

Although Rube won 155 games during his 15-year career with the Philadelphia Athletics and Boston Red Sox, he could never escape the stigma of being belted by Ruth for all those round-trippers. When he died in 1978 at age 82, Rube's obituary writer called him "Babe Ruth's favorite 'patsy.'"

Most teeth knocked out of a fan's mouth by a pitcher

4 teeth
Jack Powell, St. Louis Browns   1908

Browns hurler Jack Powell had perfect control—and he showed just how good it was when he silenced a fan with a special pitch.

A certain group of fans had been tormenting Powell all afternoon. He ignored the ragging for as long as he could. Then he finally blew his top and fired a fastball right at the head of the heckler who was leading the chorus of raspberries.

53

Thanks to Powell's great control, the ball whammed the shrieking fan James Gleason, right in the kisser, and blasted out four of his front teeth.

Gleason walked out of the stadium and right into court, where he sued Powell. But after listening to Powell's side of the story, a jury decided the pitcher's action was justified and let him go scot-free.

Most consecutive batters beaned at the start of a game

3 batters
Dock Ellis, Pittsburgh Pirates   1974

Dock Ellis collected three hits in the first inning of a 1974 game against the Cincinnati Reds. Unfortunately, he was pitching at the time and the hits were of the Reds' first three batters.

The first two pitches from the Pirates' hurler to lead-off man Pete Rose sent Rose sprawling in the dirt. The next pitch nailed him in the butt, leaving a big bruise. Rose picked up the ball, flipped it to Ellis, and trotted down to first base. "What else could I do, cry?" Rose said later. "It saved me the embarrassment of rubbing it."

Joe Morgan was Ellis's next victim. The first pitch to Morgan hit him in the shoulder and he took his base, moving Rose to second.

Next up was Danny Driessen, who got whacked with Ellis's first pitch, which loaded the bases with hit batsmen.

Ellis failed to nail cleanup hitter Tony Perez, who

deftly dodged all four high inside fastballs to draw a run-producing walk.

Ellis twice threw high and tight to the next batter, Johnny Bench, narrowly missing him, too. Finally, for everyone's safety, Pirates manager Danny Murtaugh yanked Ellis, who threw 11 pitches, all of which missed the strike zone; three of which hit human flesh.

Said Cincy manager Sparky Anderson, "No one would be crazy enough to deliberately hit the first three men. He was so wild he just didn't know where the ball was going."

Smallest shoe size of a major league pitcher

Size 3
Art Herring, Detroit Tigers—Brooklyn Dodgers—
Chicago White Sox—Pittsburgh Pirates   1929–1934,
1939, 1944–1947

Finding shoes to fit pitcher Art Herring was a big job. He was "sole" owner of the tiniest tootsies ever possessed by any full-time big-league player—an itty-bitty size 3.

Four different major league teams heard the patter of his little feet as the 5-foot-7, 168-pound hurler was shipped around the majors and minors. After five seasons with Detroit he played for the Dodgers, White Sox, Dodgers again, and Pirates, compiling a mediocre career record of 34 wins and 38 losses.

Another curious set of little feet was owned by outfielder Myril Hoag. He played for the New York Yankees, St. Louis Browns, Chicago White Sox, and Cleveland Indians between 1931 and 1945. The 5-foot-

11, 180-pound Hoag wore a size 4 shoe on one foot—
and size 4½ on the other!

Most consecutive home runs given up with the
same ball

2 homers
Johnny Allen, Brooklyn Dodgers   1943

No pitcher threw a more cursed ball than Johnny
Allen. The Dodgers hurler gave up back-to-back
homers—with the same ball!

Allen was on the mound against the Chicago Cubs
at Wrigley Field on July 30, 1943, when batter Phil
Cavarretta walloped the ball into a screen high above
the right-field bleachers for a round-tripper.

The ball caromed off the screen onto the field, so the
umpire-in-chief left it in the game. Allen then fired the
same ball to batter Bill Nicholson—who also pounded
it over the wall for a homer. Since Nicholson's shot
sailed out of the park, Allen was mercifully spared the
chance of serving three straight home runs off the same
ball.

That was the last ball Allen ever threw for the Dodgers. He was traded to the New York Giants the very
next day.

Farthest pitch thrown out of the strike zone to be called a strike

4 feet
Wild Bill Donovan, Detroit Tigers   1909

Wild Bill Donovan threw a pitch that was so wide the batter couldn't have hit it with a telephone pole, but plate umpire Tim Hurst called it a strike anyway.

The veteran Detroit Tigers hurler was pitching to the Philadelphia Athletics' Eddie Collins during a 1909 game when catcher Boss Schmidt signaled for a pitchout. Donovan thought Schmidt was losing his mind because the bases were empty and he already had two strikes on Collins.

The pitcher waved off Schmidt's signal. But the catcher repeated it. Puzzled, Donovan called him out to the mound for a conference.

"What the hell are you doin'?" Donovan whispered.

"Just do as I say," Schmidt responded. "Eddie's been cussin' out Hurst, and Hurst just warned him that the next one's goin' to be a strike no matter where it is."

So Donovan threw the next pitch four feet out of the strike zone—and Hurst shouted, "Stee-rike threeee!"

A Comedy of Errors
WARPED RECORDS OF FIELDERS

Most wild throws to home plate by an outfielder on one play

2 wild throws
Bing Miller, Philadelphia Athletics 1928

On one wacky play, A's right fielder Bing Miller twice wanted to go home with his throws. But both times they ended up in another neighborhood.

In a 1928 game, St. Louis Browns runner Frank O'Rourke was on second base when batter Heinie Manush drilled a sharp single to right field. Miller, determined to make a play at the plate, scooped up the ball, juggled it as if it was too hot to handle, and then cut loose with a strong throw.

Unfortunately, his peg sailed yards over the head of catcher Mickey Cochrane, allowing O'Rourke to score. Getting the ball on the rebound from the grandstand, Cochrane threw to second hoping to nail Manush, who was trying to advance on Miller's errant throw. But Manush slid into second safely as the ball bounced off the glove of shortstop Jimmy Dykes.

Manush picked himself up and took off for third. The ball rolled into right field where Miller repeated his hot-potato act. He juggled the ball between his glove and his bare hand for so long that Manush headed for the plate.

Once again, Miller fired home. Once again, he hurled it wildly over the catcher's head. And once again, a St. Louis runner scored easily.

After watching this fielding botchery, Browns third base coach Jimmy Austin rushed to the dugout, grabbed a pail of water, raced over to the ball, and doused it. As the crowd roared with laughter, Austin shouted, "There, that should cool off the damn thing!"

Last player to catch a pop-up in his cap and get away with it

Luis Aparicio, Baltimore Orioles   1967

Orioles shortstop Luis Aparicio used the old hat trick to snag a pop fly.

Baltimore was playing the Boston Red Sox in Fenway Park when a high pop-up was hit to short left field. Aparicio back-pedaled until he was under the ball and then reached up to flip down his sunglasses because he was staring right into the bright July sun.

But Little Looie flipped too hard, and his sunglasses and hat plopped into his glove. A split-second later the ball landed smack-dab in his cap, which was resting in his glove.

The rule book prohibits intentionally catching a ball with a cap, but umpire Bill Kinnamon ruled the catch was legal because Aparicio hadn't done it on purpose.

Most runs kicked in by an outfielder

3 runs
Zack Wheat, Brooklyn Dodgers   1916

Dodgers outfielder Zack Wheat booted the equivalent of a field goal in a September 1916 game against the Philadelphia Phillies—scoring three "points" when he kicked the ball into the stands!

Unfortunately, the trio of runs went on the Phillies' side of the scoreboard—and Wheat's kick cost the Dodgers a game they should have won.

Brooklyn was winning, 4–2, in the eighth inning when the Phillies rallied and put two men on base. That brought up dangerous hitter Gavvy "Cactus" Cravath.

Cravath lashed a line drive straight toward Wheat. The outfielder raced in, expecting to catch the ball on the first bounce. But it hit a pebble and took a weird hop toward the toe of Wheat's right foot—just as his foot was swinging forward.

To everyone's amazement, the impact sent the ball sailing backwards over Wheat's shoulder and into the bleachers behind him! The umpires ruled Cravath's hit a three-run homer.

Philadelphia won the game, 5–4. The Dodgers lost not by a nose, but by a toe!

Longest time a double-play combo refused to speak to each other

22 years
Joe Tinker, Johnny Evers, Chicago Cubs   1908–1930

Everybody knows baseball's most famous double-play combination was "Tinker to Evers to Chance." But what most fans may not know is that shortstop Joe Tinker and second baseman Johnny Evers hated each other so much they never exchanged a word off the field from 1908 to 1930!

Oddly enough, Tinker and Evers had been best friends when they began playing regularly together on the Cubs in 1903. But one day in 1908, Tinker got upset when Evers took a taxi to the ballpark and never offered him a ride. The two quarreled about the perceived slight, then stopped speaking to each other.

For the next five years, until Tinker was traded to a different team, they remained the same slick double-play combo but spoke to each other only on the field and only if it was absolutely necessary.

Tinker and Evers didn't talk to each other for 22 years. But the silence finally was broken in 1930, long after both had retired, when they unexpectedly ran into each other at a Chicago radio station.

Recalled Evers: "At the sight of each other, we had that old feeling again—meaning we wanted to fight. We started toward each other, and what do you think happened? When we got within punching distance we threw our arms around each other and cried like a couple of babies."

And the players who had been the most famous double-play combo in baseball history were friends once again.

Most times an infielder snapped his fingers in disgust in an inning

3 times
Stan Hack, Chicago Cubs   1932

Aging Cubs pitcher Burleigh Grimes had almost no zip left on his fastball by 1932, so the old man didn't react too kindly when rookie third baseman Stan Hack made a pair of goofs that wrecked Grimes's chances of winning a game.

With a man on first, Hack eagerly went after a routine double-play grounder but accidentally booted it. He snapped his fingers in disgust—and Grimes aimed a string of X-rated insults at the young third sacker.

Then Hack failed to cleanly field a bunt and it went for an infield hit that loaded the bases. Once again, Hack angrily snapped his fingers.

Grimes swore even louder, but somehow managed to get two more outs without anyone scoring. Then he coaxed the next batter to hit a grounder to Hack for what should have ended the inning. But the rookie kicked away the ball and a run scored. Hack again snapped his fingers in disgust.

Cubs manager Rogers Hornsby went out to the mound and gave the hook to Grimes, who was now fuming mad. Before heading for the showers, the irate hurler unleashed a torrent of four-letter words. "Why take me out?" he yelled in protest. "Why not take out that guy who's only snapping his fingers at the ball?"

Only infielder to win a footrace during a game

Jake "Eagle Eye" Beckley, Cincinnati Reds 1898

Jake Beckley pumped some excitement into an otherwise dull contest by winning a footrace with an opposing base runner—during the game.

The 31-year-old veteran was playing first base for Cincinnati when Louisville Colonels rookie Tommy Leach, appearing in his first major league game, drew a walk and eagerly sprinted to the bag.

As the two stood side by side, Beckley—who outweighed the 20-year-old Leach by 50 pounds—drawled: "You may have been a speedster in the minors, son, but you're just average up here. Why, big and old as I am, I can outrun you."

Leach took that as a challenge to steal. Then Beckley walked away from first base, letting Leach take a big lead. But behind the rookie's back, Jake took several steps toward second base. The moment the pitcher wound up, the youngster bounded for second. So did Beckley.

Having given himself a big edge, Jake slid into second base well ahead of the startled Leach. Said Beckley with a grin to the rookie: "Never saw that kind of running in the minors, did you?"

Most name changes by a shortstop

3 name changes
Jose Uribe, St. Louis Cardinals–San Francisco
Giants 1984–1990

Jose Uribe changed names more often than a bank robber featured on TV's "America's Most Wanted."

While playing with the minor league Louisville Redbirds, he was just plain Jose Gonzalez. But shortly after he moved up to the bigs, the shortstop decided there were too many Jose Gonzalezes in baseball. He wanted a less common name, so he started calling himself Uribe Gonzalez.

But that monicker didn't last long, so he changed it again—to Jose Uribe.

Giants coach Rocky Bridges, noting that Uribe had joined the team via a trade, quipped: "In that trade, he truly was the player to be named later."

Most consecutive balls missed by a catcher

23 balls
Billy Sullivan, Chicago White Sox 1910

White Sox pitcher Ed Walsh was famed for his control, but his catcher Billy Sullivan missed 23 straight balls that were tossed by the hurler. No wonder. Walsh was throwing them more than 500 feet straight down!

On the morning of August 10, 1910, Walsh stood at a window near the top of the Washington Monument and began hurling baseballs one at a time to Sullivan on the ground below.

Sullivan figured he'd easily snag most of the missiles. But a stiff wind kept whipping the balls away from him—and out of the first 23 tossed, he didn't even come close to catching a single one.

Sullivan was tired from chasing the balls when suddenly the breeze let up. And as the next ball came hurtling down, he finally got his glove under it and caught the ball. For the day, Sullivan snared one out of Walsh's 24 tosses in a monumentally poor performance.

There's a footnote to this record. A few minutes after Walsh tossed the balls, fellow hurler Doc White threw down 15 balls to Sullivan, who managed to catch two of them. White then turned to Walsh and said, "I always did contend that my control was better than yours."

Longest run by an infielder to tag a runner who was already out

250 feet (est.)
Mark Koenig, New York Yankees   1930

Yankees shortstop Mark Koenig got the out, but runner Mule Haas got the last laugh.

In a 1930 game between New York and the Philadelphia Athletics at Shibe Park, the A's had runners on first and third and one out. The next batter hit a made-to-order double-play grounder to second baseman Tony Lazzeri. He scooped up the ball and flipped it to Koenig who tagged second and fired to first for the inning-ending twin killing.

First baseman Lou Gehrig rolled the ball toward the mound as his fellow Yankees began trotting off the field. Meanwhile, Haas, who was the runner forced at second, thought he was safe at second—even though he wasn't—and continued to dash around the bases. Sensing something was wrong, Koenig raced to the mound, picked up the ball, and chased after Haas.

Haas crossed home plate and headed for the dugout when he saw Koenig running toward him. Haas then let Koenig chase him into and out of the dugout and to the coach's box before getting tagged. Recalled Yankees pitcher Lefty Gomez, "Both clubs had a good laugh at Mark's expense. That was the longest and toughest nonout that Mark ever got."

Most energy-conserving outfielder in major league history

Heinie Manush, Detroit Tigers–St. Louis Browns–Washington Senators–Boston Red Sox–Brooklyn Dodgers–Pittsburgh Pirates   1923–1939

Heinie Manush was a man ahead of his time. Long before it became fashionable, he was conserving energy—his own.

During the dog days of summer, the left fielder took extra steps to save his energy—by not taking steps. When his team came up to bat, and he wasn't scheduled to hit, he often didn't even return to the dugout. He would amble over to the left-field bleachers, open the gate, and sit down with the fans until it was time for him to take the field again.

"Why the hell should I walk 200-some feet to the dugout when the bleachers are right behind me?" he once told a reporter.

Manush's energy-saving tactics paid off. He played

17 years in the majors, compiled a lifetime batting average of .330, and was elected to the Baseball Hall of Fame in 1964.

Most bases given up by a catcher on a passed ball

3 bases
Ernie Lombardi, New York Giants   1943

Giants catcher Ernie Lombardi was so slow-footed that coaches could clock him with a sundial.

His slothlike speed was never more apparent than during a 1943 game against the Pittsburgh Pirates at Forbes Field.

With the Pirates holding on to an 8–7 lead in the bottom of the eighth inning, Vince DiMaggio singled for Pittsburgh.

The next pitch to batter Pete Coscarart, got away from Lombardi for a passed ball and rolled toward the backstop. While the catcher lumbered after the ball, the fleet-footed DiMaggio scampered to second base. When DiMaggio saw that Lombardi had yet to retrieve the ball, the Pirate runner raced to third.

Meanwhile, Giants pitcher Bill Sayles was so shocked that DiMaggio had reached third, the hurler forgot to cover home. Seeing the plate unguarded and knowing he could crawl faster than Lombardi could run, DiMaggio trotted home—capping a play in which he advanced three bases on a passed ball!

That run proved to be the winning one in a 9–8 Pirates victory.

Most passed balls charged to a *pitcher*

6 passed balls
Harry "Rube" Vickers, Cincinnati Reds   1902

In one of the screwiest games ever, Cincinnati hurler Rube Vickers did the catching while outfielders did the pitching—and the whole Reds team turned the game into a travesty.

Even a Little League benchwarmer could have done a better job of catching than Vickers did that day. He committed six passed balls, setting a record that still stands.

On the last day of the 1902 season, the Reds wanted to cancel their game with the Pirates because the field in Pittsburgh was muddy and the day was cold. But Pirates owner Barney Dreyfuss refused. Forced to play, peeved Reds manager Joe Kelley turned the game into a joke.

He shifted his men around to positions they'd never played before. Vickers went behind the plate, while two outfielders and a first baseman rotated on the mound. Kelley also put three left-handers in the infield.

Vickers was in his clowning glory as catcher. He made little effort to catch pitches that strayed too far from the strike zone. Teammates roared with laughter as he casually strolled after each of his six passed balls. Once, Vickers even pulled out a handkerchief and loudly blew his nose while going after one of the balls.

Thanks to Cincinnati's show of farce, Pittsburgh won, 11–2. But the fans were so infuriated by the debacle that Pirates owner Dreyfuss refunded all their money to keep them from wrecking the stadium.

Most times that a catcher was conked on the head during a game

3 times
Rollie Hemsley, Cleveland Indians   1940

In his 19 years in the bigs, Rollie Hemsley caught in nearly 1,500 games. But none was as painful as the one in which the hard-to-hurt backstop got cracked on the skull by a bat and two foul tips.

Early in a game against the Philadelphia Athletics, a foul tip slammed into Hemsley's head with such force that he was knocked to the ground. He got up seeing stars and momentarily forgetting his name, but Rollie went back to work behind the plate..

A bit later, A's batter Benny McCoy swung so hard at a pitch that he spun completely around and his bat whacked Hemsley on the back of the head. The catcher went down again. Struggling to his feet, he saw the umpire holding up a couple of dozen fingers.

Hemsley recovered a few moments later and insisted on staying in the game. He was still woozy when another foul tip conked him on his already-bruised noggin. Once again, he fell to the ground, and forgot his name. Rollie shook off his third head-bonk of the day and finished the game.

After watching the hard-headed catcher, a sportswriter said: "No wonder there's a shortage of good catchers. Any guy smart enough to become a good catcher is also smart enough not to!"

Cleverest questioning of a plate umpire's call

Ray Murray, Philadelphia Athletics   1952

In 1952, the league office announced that catchers who turned around and questioned the plate umpire about balls and strikes risked getting thrown out of the game.

So A's catcher Ray Murray—not one to stifle his opinions—came up with a clever solution. He wrote a message on a business card, showed it to manager Jimmy Dykes, who approved of what it said, and stuffed it in his back pocket for use when needed.

In the next game, plate umpire Larry Napp called a ball on a pitch that Murray was convinced was a strike. But Murray didn't turn around and squawk. Instead, he took the card out of his pocket and, while still crouched and looking straight ahead at the pitcher, handed it to Napp.

The card read, "Mr. Dykes and the pitcher and I would like to know where the last pitch was."

Recalled Murray, "Napp just broke out laughing. He didn't do anything to me because I didn't turn around when I gave him the card.

"Somebody made up a story that the business card was that of an optometrist. If that had been true, I would have been long gone."

Costliest routine toss from the catcher to the pitcher

Rollie Hemsley to Bob Feller, Cleveland Indians 1940

Pitching great Bob Feller picked the wrong time to daydream while facing the New York Yankees—and it cost the poor Feller the game.

The score was tied, 0–0, in the eighth inning when Yankee slugger Joe DiMaggio came to the plate with teammate Red Rolfe perched on third base. Feller's first two pitches were wide. After the second one, catcher Rollie Hemsley fired the ball back to Feller.

But the pitcher's mind had wandered off into the clouds and he didn't see the ball coming until it was too late. Feller frantically stabbed for the ball but it skidded off his glove and shot out into center field.

Rolfe raced in from third base to score—and the Yankees won, 1–0, thanks to Feller's embarrassing daydream.

Most bases allowed a runner while holding the ball

3 bases
Zack Taylor, Brooklyn Dodgers 1923

Dodgers catcher Zack Taylor was throwing a temper tantrum and holding the ball instead of holding his temper and throwing the ball. As a result, the boiling-mad backstop allowed a runner to score all the way from first base.

In the second inning of a September 8, 1923, game with Boston, the Braves had runners Stuffy McInnis on third and Hod Ford on second with Bob Smith at the plate.

Smith swatted a single, scoring McInnis and Ford. But Taylor began furiously arguing with umpire Hank O'Day that Ford had run out of the base path. While the squabble raged on, Smith dashed from first to second. Seeing that Taylor's back still was turned, he then raced to third.

And as the hot-headed catcher continued to berate the ump, Smith came romping across the plate. Taylor's right of free speech had given Boston a free run.

Most wild throws on a bunt in All-Star Game history

2 wild throws
Joe DiMaggio, Jimmie Foxx, American League   1938

A dinky little bunt by Leo Durocher wound up as a two-run "four-bagger"—thanks to back-to-back wild throws by two of baseball's biggest stars, Joe DiMaggio and Jimmie Foxx.

In the seventh inning of the 1938 All-Star Game, the National League had a 2–0 lead with the Cincinnati Reds' Frank McCormick on first base. Durocher, the Brooklyn Dodgers' shortstop, laid a bunt down the third-base line. Foxx, playing third base instead of his normal first base for the Boston Red Sox, scooped up the ball and whistled it toward first—but his throw sailed wildly into right field.

As McCormick and Durocher romped around the

bases, New York Yankees outfielder DiMaggio ran down the ball and frantically threw it toward home plate. But his peg soared high over catcher Bill Dickey's outstretched hands—and both runners crossed the plate.

Foxx and DiMaggio were each charged with an error. Thanks to their help, the National League won, 4–1.

Commenting on the American League's four errors in the game, Yankees hurler Lefty Gomez quipped, "It was an All-Star game, all right—all the stars made errors."

Longest distance a superstar was deliberately knocked off his feet by a teammate

5 feet
Lou Gehrig, New York Yankees   1926

Big Lou Gehrig played college football, but the "Iron Horse" never took a gridiron hit that jolted him as much as a tooth-rattling block laid on him by a teammate.

What's more, the fellow Yankee did it on purpose—to save Lou from an even worse fate.

The Yankees were playing the Brooklyn Dodgers in a 1926 exhibition game in Waycross, Georgia, when Dodger batter Bill Marriott hit a pop-up between home plate and first base. Gehrig and Yankee catcher Pat Collins both ran for the ball, each unaware of what the other was doing.

Pitcher Sad Sam Jones saw to his horror that a collision between the two solidly packed men was inevitable. So Jones threw his 170-pound body right into the 200-pound Gehrig. The tremendous crash sent Gehrig flying through the air. He landed in foul territory five feet away while Collins made the catch. Struggling to his feet, Gehrig stared at Jones with a look of bewilderment. The pitcher rushed over and quickly explained why he had bowled him over.

"I didn't know you ever played football," Gehrig said.

"I never did," Jones replied.

Gehrig, checking for bruises, mumbled, "You sure should have."

Only outfielder to catch his own home run

Dixie Walker, Pittsburgh Pirates   1949

It sounds like a feat only Superman could accomplish, but Dixie Walker once walloped a home run, rounded the bases, then ran out to right field and caught the ball!

Impossible? Nope. But of course, there was a catch to Dixie's catch.

When he slammed his round-tripper, the ball stuck in the screen above right-center field at Brooklyn's Ebbets Field. It stayed there until the Pirates were retired that inning and Dixie had returned to his outfield position. Then he went over and yanked on the screen to shake loose his home-run ball—and caught it.

Longest distance a glove was thrown to get a runner out

7 feet
Terry Mulholland, San Francisco Giants   1986

In a game against the New York Mets on September 3, 1986, Giants rookie hurler Terry Mulholland fielded a hard smash off the bat of Keith Hernandez. Mulholland whirled to throw to first base—but couldn't get the baseball out of his brand-new glove.

Mulholland clawed at the ball, but it was firmly stuck in the webbing. Frantically, he began racing Hernandez to first. However, the pitcher quickly realized that the Mets' batter was going to beat him.

So seven feet from the bag, Mulholland alertly flipped his glove—with the ball still stuck inside—to shocked first baseman Bob Brenly.

"The first thing I looked for was to get the ball," said Brenly. "I wasn't sure if there was a rule that said I had to hold the ball, and not just the ball in the glove."

The umpire ruled that the play was legal—and Hernandez was out by a glove.

Most bases allowed a runner by an infielder who was being chased by a horse

4 bases
Cap Anson, Chicago Cubs   1892

The Louisville Colonels beat the Chicago Cubs in an 1892 game because of horseplay—literally.

On one wacky play, there were nine Cubs and a *horse* on the field. Nope, the nag—named Sam—hadn't been sent up from a farm team. He belonged to the Cubs' groundskeeper, who used Sam to pull a lawnmower. When Sam wasn't working, he stayed in a little corral beyond the outfield fence.

During the Colonels-Cubs game, Louisville slugger Tom Brown slapped a grounder to Cubs shortstop Bill Dahlen. But Dahlen's throw to first baseman Cap Anson was wide, and the ball ricocheted off the grandstand wall into right field.

Anson went chasing after the ball when suddenly he saw a huge white sway-backed equine galloping hell-bent for leather straight at him. Somebody had forgotten to close the gate to Sam's corral! And the horse, who for some reason had always hated Anson, went after the first baseman with a vengeance.

Anson forgot about the ball and concentrated on running for his life with Sam close behind. Meanwhile, batter Tom Brown was running around the bases. While Anson managed to get away from the horse, Brown managed to score the run that won the game.

Most outs from a ball that bounced off a fielder's noggin

3 outs
Odell Hale, Cleveland Indians   1935

The weirdest triple play ever was set up when a player accidentally got beaned on the head.

During a game against the Cleveland Indians on September 7, 1935, the Boston Red Sox loaded the bases with no outs in the bottom of the ninth and Joe Cronin at bat.

Cronin smashed a line drive straight at Indians third

baseman Odell Hale. The ball whacked Hale in the forehead and ricocheted right to shortstop Billy Knickerbocker—who caught it on the fly for out No. 1. Knickerbocker then fired the ball to second baseman Roy Hughes, who stepped on the bag to double up the runner for out No. 2. Next, Hughes whipped the ball to Hal Trosky at first for out No. 3.

It was an amazing triple play—started by Hale's heads-up fielding.

Getting the Run Around

WARPED RECORDS
OF BASE RUNNERS

Most home runs negated in a year
by daydreaming

2 homers
Babe Herman, Brooklyn Dodgers   1930

Because Dodgers flake Babe Herman didn't pay attention, his team had to pay the price. Two Brooklyn home runs were wiped out in 1930 thanks to Babe.

In both cases, the batter was declared out for passing Herman on the base path—while Babe was dawdling along with his head in the clouds, watching the ball fly overhead.

On May 30th, Del Bissonette smashed a pitch over

the wall and started racing around the bases. Bissonette, looking forward to rousing congratulations at home plate, shot past the slow-moving Herman without even seeing him.

Then, on September 15th, Glenn "Buckshot" Wright hit an apparent homer with Herman on base. And once again, Herman dillydallied long enough to watch his teammate run past him.

Years later, when reminded how his baserunning boners had negated two homers, Herman reportedly said, "I never could figure out what their hurry was."

Greatest distance a batter walked to first on a base-on-balls

230 feet
Jack Fournier, St. Louis Cardinals   1922

Jack Fournier took the scenic route during a bizarre at-bat—he went from the bench to the plate to first base to the bench to first base to the bench!

The Cardinals first baseman drew a walk while pinch-hitting against the Chicago Cubs and ambled to the bag. But as soon as he got there, Fournier saw teammate Leslie Mann coming in to run for him, so he trotted back to the bench.

But just as Mann got close to the bag, Cubs catcher Bob O'Farrell fired the ball to first baseman Ray Grimes, who tagged Mann.

"You're out!" shouted umpire Cy Rigler.

The St. Louis bench emptied as furious Cards surrounded Rigler, demanding to know how he could call Mann out before the guy was even officially in the game.

80

As the brouhaha went on, Fournier thought, "If Mann isn't in the game, I must be!" So he left the bench, casually strolled past the squabblers, and took his base again.

Once in place, Fournier declared. "I'm still in the game and I'm on first base!"

Rigler took one look at the runner, reversed his earlier call, and said, "Mann isn't out because he isn't in the game, and Fournier isn't out because nobody has tagged him."

Cardinals manager Branch Rickey then sent Mann back out again to run for Fournier—who returned to the bench to complete a record 230-foot trek to first base on a walk.

Longest elapsed time before getting thrown out at first on a tap to the mound

35 seconds
Bobo Newsom, New York Yankees 1947

After tapping back to the mound, Bobo Newsom took a detour on his way to first base that had the fans rolling in the aisles.

The much-traveled hurler was making his first start for the Yankees in a 1947 game against the Chicago White Sox at Comiskey Park. In his first trip to the plate in the third inning, Newsom hit an easy grounder back to the mound, where it was cleanly fielded by Sox pitcher Joe Haynes.

But rather than run it out, Newsom trotted directly to the New York dugout on the first-base side. Meanwhile, Haynes refused to toss the ball to first baseman Rudy York for the routine out.

But just as Haynes was getting ready to face batter Snuffy Stirnweiss, Newsom crawled furtively like a big cat from the Yankees' bench. Then he bolted suddenly in a mad dash for first base. York shouted to Haynes, who fired to first just in time to retire Newsom—more than a half minute after he had hit the ball.

Said Bobo with a wink after the game, "Since I can't fool 'em with my speed, I thought I'd hoodwink 'em with my cunning."

Most times duped by the hidden-ball trick in one day

2 times
Rabbit Maranville, Boston Braves   1916

Rabbit Maranville felt like crawling in a rabbit hole when New York Giants second baseman Larry Doyle tagged him out in a 1916 game by using the oldest sucker play in the book—the hidden-ball trick.

Teammates razzed Rabbit unmercifully the rest of the game. But then they quit, and the relieved Boston Brave thought he'd heard the last of it.

That evening, as Rabbit and some teammates were dining at their hotel, another player raved about the chef's "special" dessert that wasn't on the menu. Rabbit promptly ordered it, and the waiter brought him a huge mound of ice cream topped with fresh cherries and whipped cream.

Rabbit dug in with gusto—and dug out a baseball hidden inside. His teammates had given him his just desserts!

Longest run around the bases backwards

360 feet
Jimmy Piersall, New York Mets   1963

When Jimmy Piersall slapped his 100th major league homer on June 23, 1963, spectators cheered—then cracked up laughing as he celebrated by taking the wackiest round-trip ever.

The silly center fielder backpedaled to first while facing home plate, then rounded the turn and went on to second and third.

And when he finished circling the bases, Piersall slid backwards into home plate!

Interestingly, it was the only home run that Piersall ever hit in the National League. (He played all but 40 games in the American League in his 17-year career.)

Although everyone in the ballpark, including the opposing Philadelphia Phillies, laughed at his antics, league officials were not amused. They enacted a new rule requiring runners to face the bases.

Oldest player not in the lineup to steal a base

47 years old
Phil Niekro, Cleveland Indians   1986

After more than two decades in the majors, Phil Niekro had done everything in baseball except steal a base. But at the age of 47, he finally stole one—though he wasn't even in the game.

Niekro "stole" the first base of his career in the eighth inning of an October 4, 1986, game between the

Indians and the Seattle Mariners in Cleveland. The Indians were at bat and leading, 5–2, with a man on first. Suddenly, Niekro burst out of the Indians' dugout wearing a red bandanna over his face. He raced straight toward second base and made a diving headfirst slide into the bag. Niekro looked up at umpire Vic Voltaggio, who shouted: "Safe!"

The pitcher then yanked the bag out of the ground and sprinted back to the dugout with the base tucked under his arm as 12,000 delighted fans cheered.

Longest home-run trot

5 minutes
Zack Wheat, Brooklyn Dodgers   1926

A home-run trot by aging Dodgers outfielder Zack Wheat turned into a long, interrupted journey.

With the St. Louis Cardinals leading, 9–5, in the bottom of the 10th inning at Ebbets Field in 1926, Zack stepped to the plate and slammed the ball over the right-field fence.

But as he trotted toward second base, Zack's old legs—which had more mileage on them than a used car bought at Honest John's—suddenly gave out. He dropped to the ground next to the bag at second. The team trainer, the manager, and his teammates rushed out of the dugout and crowded solicitously around him. It appeared that he had severely pulled a muscle.

Brooklyn manager Wilbert Robinson suggested sending in a pinch runner. But the grizzled 18-year veteran refused. It was, after all, *his* home run and he was determined to finish rounding the bases.

The game was delayed for nearly five minutes as Zack sat on second. Finally he struggled to his feet and, to the heartfelt cheers of the Brooklyn fans, he painfully hobbled home. It was the last home run Zack Wheat ever hit for the Dodgers.

Biggest crowd to eyeball a baserunner's jock strap

15,000 fans
Steve Lyons, Chicago White Sox   1990

In the silliest attempt by a player to air his dirty laundry, Steve Lyons dropped his drawers at first base—exposing his jock strap for all to see.

Following a headfirst slide into the bag during a game at Tigers Stadium in Detroit, the White Sox utility man found his pants full of dirt. So he calmly and unthinkingly pulled them down to his ankles and started brushing the dirt off his legs.

His athletic supporter and shorts were clearly visible to the 15,000 fans in the stands, and also to a TV audience because a camera was trained right on him at the time. Not until the crowd roared with laughter did Lyons remember where he was and quickly pull up his pants.

When the embarrassed player eventually returned to the dugout, giggling women in the stands waved money at him and one man offered Lyons his belt.

Asked later about his nutty behavior, Lyons, whom his teammates call "Psycho," lamely explained, "I'm still not sure why I did it. I just kind of forgot where I was."

First runner ever to steal *first* base

Fred Tenney, New York Giants   1908

The St. Louis Cardinals didn't know whether Giants runner Fred Tenney was coming or going. During a game July 31, 1908, he swiped second base—but on the next play, he turned around and "stole" first base!

The first steal of first was just an attempt to confuse the Cardinals.

Tenney was on first and teammate Dummy Taylor on third when Tenney took off for second. St. Louis pitcher Bugs Raymond threw the ball to third hoping to catch Taylor straying from the bag. But Taylor stayed put as Tenney slid safely into second.

On the next pitch, Tenney unexpectedly turned around and dashed back toward first in a wacky attempt to draw a throw so that Taylor could run home. But Raymond was so dumbfounded he just stood and watched Tenney "steal" first. A shocked Taylor never moved off third.

Incredibly, on the following pitch Tenney took off for second—and stole that base again!

Five weeks later, Germany Schaefer, of the Detroit Tigers, pulled the same stunt by "stealing" first base. The play was soon declared illegal because it made a mockery of the game.

Most opposing players bowled over during one trip around the bases

3 players
Bill Lange, Chicago Cubs   1896

Outfielder Bill Lange was a wrecking ball on legs. Six feet, 1½ inches tall and 200 pounds of muscle, he delighted in toppling infielders like tenpins as he roared around the bases.

In an 1896 game against the Pittsburgh Pirates, Lange turned a simple grounder to third into a "home run" by knocking down three Pirates who happened to be in his path.

As Lange raced toward first, Pittsburgh third baseman Denny Lyons scooped up the ball and fired it to first baseman Jake Beckley. But Lange rammed Beckley with such tremendous force that the first sacker was sent sprawling and the ball flew into right field.

Lange rampaged toward second, shouting, "Look out, here I come!" He arrived at second just as the ball came to shortstop Bones Ely, who had rushed over to cover the base. The collision knocked Ely silly and the ball loose.

Lange barreled on to third, where he plowed into Lyons, and then raced safely home. Groused Pirates catcher Joe Sugden, "Lange must think he's playing rugby."

Longest throw by a base runner

230 feet
Eddie Stanky, Brooklyn Dodgers   1944

Eddie Stanky made a dynamite throw on a double play. But there was one problem. He was the *runner*, not the fielder.

In a 1944 game against the St. Louis Cardinals at Ebbets Field, the Brooklyn Dodgers held a slim 2–1 lead in the bottom of the sixth inning. With Bobby Bragan the runner on first, Stanky lashed a line drive to right field where Stan Musial made a spectacular, diving catch.

Bragan, who was running on the play, was halfway to third base when Musial caught the ball. So the right fielder got to his feet and threw toward first baseman Ray Sanders, hoping to double up Bragan.

But Sanders never caught the ball. As the throw came into the infield, Stanky, who had rounded first, snared the toss with his bare hand and then, in disgust, fired the ball against the right field wall 230 feet away from where he stood.

Umpire Larry Goetz called Bragan out anyway for Stanky's interference. Then he turned to Stanky and said, "Save those throws for when you take the field."

Most runners on the same base at the same time

3 runners
Babe Herman, Chick Fewster, Dazzy Vance
Brooklyn Dodgers   1926

In a scene that should have been in a Three Stooges flick, three Dodgers wound up on third base simultaneously.

The zany "triple play" came after Brooklyn loaded the bases with one out in the seventh inning of a 1–1 game against the Boston Braves in 1926. Hank DeBerry was on third, Dazzy Vance on second, and Chick Fewster on first when batter Babe Herman blasted a drive to right field for a sure double and possible triple.

DeBerry scored. But Vance waited on second until he saw the ball ricochet off the wall before he started plodding slowly toward third. By then Fewster was breathing down his neck—followed closely by Herman, who had already rounded second and was running with his head down.

Coach Mickey O'Neill saw disaster looming and yelled at Herman, "Back! Back!" But Vance, who was headed toward home plate, thought the coach was talking to him. So he hurried back to third, arriving just as Fewster got there!

A split-second later, Herman chugged into third to make it three on a bag.

Fewster figured he was out and trotted off toward the dugout. Meanwhile, the ball had reached Braves third baseman Eddie Taylor—who tagged everybody he could reach. Then for good measure, second baseman Doc Gautreau snatched the ball, chased down Fewster, and tagged him, too!

The umpires ruled Vance was safe at third since he got there first. Fewster was out because he had been tagged and Herman was out for passing Fewster on the base path. Incredibly, Herman had doubled into a double play!

Said disgusted Dodgers manager Wilbert Robinson, "That's the first time those guys got together on anything all season."

Most expensive dirty baserunning trick

$5,000
Arlie Latham, St. Louis Browns   1889

Brooklyn fans rioted and threatened to beat up the Browns after St. Louis base runner Arlie Latham cut across the infield to score from second—while the umpire's back was turned.

But Latham's cheap scam proved expensive for his team's owner—$5,000, which was a king's ransom a century ago.

In the top of the ninth inning of a tie game in Brooklyn, Latham was the runner on second base when player-manager Charlie Comiskey laid down a bunt.

"The play was close at first, but they got Comiskey," recalled Latham. "While the umpire—there was only one arbitrator in those days—was looking at the close finish at first, I cut third base by 20 feet and was nearing the plate just as the decision was made at first.

"I was called safe at home. The crowd roared, and the Brooklyn club officials came onto the field to tell the umpire I had cut third. Of course, he hadn't seen me do it, so all he could do was allow the run, which proved to be the winning run. After the game, we were pelted with rocks and sticks when we got into our bus. It was a nasty riot."

The Browns were scheduled to play the Dodgers again the next day. But Latham's short-circuit of third base caused such an uproar in Brooklyn that Browns owner Chris von der Ahe refused to let his team even go to the ballpark.

The owner forfeited his share of the gate receipts— $3,500—and was fined $1,500 by the league for failing to place his team on the field. But von der Ahe felt losing $5,000 was less painful than having his team get beat up.

Farthest distance a ball bounced off a base runner's head

55 feet
Chuck Klein, Philadelphia Phillies   1932

The hardest skull in baseball belonged to Chuck Klein.

During a 1932 game against the visiting Brooklyn Dodgers, the Philadelphia outfielder was trying to score from first base on a double. Dodgers first baseman George Kelly caught the throw from the outfield and whipped a strong relay peg to home.

As Klein slid into the plate, the throw smacked him right in the head. The ball ricocheted off Klein's noggin and soared all the way into the grandstand's sixth row, where it broke the pince-nez specs of a startled elderly fan.

To the crowd's shock, Klein not only wasn't killed,

91

he wasn't hurt. He immediately bounced to his feet and flashed a wide grin—he never even rubbed his head!

The stupendous blow didn't bother the iron-skulled Philly one bit. In fact, Klein went on to slam a homer, a triple, and two singles. In the field, he made seven putouts and one assist.

The next day, Klein's teammates offered to take turns throwing balls at his head!

New Kids on the (Chopping) Block

WARPED RECORDS OF ROOKIES

Only pitcher to give up a single, double, triple, and homer in his debut inning

Al Grunwald, Pittsburgh Pirates   1955

It's one thing to hit for the cycle. It's quite another to *be* hit for the cycle. That's what happened to Pirates southpaw Al Grunwald in his first major league game.

He was summoned to the mound in the fourth inning of a 1955 game against the New York Giants at the Polo Grounds. The Giants were leading, 3–0, and had runners on second and third with one out.

Willie Mays welcomed Grunwald to the bigs by

whacking a 400-foot blast to right-center for a two-run triple. After Hank Thompson grounded out, Monte Irvin belted a 390-foot shot off the left-field fence for a run-scoring double. Then Don Mueller drilled a single.

Grunwald was still reeling from those hits when Whitey Lockman stepped to the plate—and clouted the ball 410 feet into the upper deck in right field for a three-run homer.

As easy as one, two, three, four, the Giants had hit for the cycle in Grunwald's first major league inning. Mercifully, Pittsburgh manager Fred Haney rescued the rookie from further trouble with the hook as the Giants scored eight runs in the frame and coasted to an easy 12–3 victory.

Grunwald made pitching appearances in just eight more games before hanging up his glove—without ever recording a win in the majors.

Only rookie to bean his manager while trying to impress him

Jack Graney, Cleveland Indians   1906

Jack Graney's pitching was legendary in his hometown of St. Thomas, Ontario. But the young sensation's first outing with Cleveland was a disaster—he beaned his own manager!

At batting practice in training camp, Graney's pitches sailed everywhere but over the plate. He grew more and more nervous because his boss, player-manager Nap Lajoie, was looking on.

"When Lajoie came up to the plate I wanted to give it everything I had because he was the manager of the team and one of baseball's greatest hitters," recalled Graney, who eventually played only one year in the bigs.

"That's all I could think about, the boys back in St. Thomas sitting around the coal stove talking about how Jack Graney struck out the great Lajoie.

"I reared back and threw the fastest ball I'd ever pitched, and instead of striking him out I *knocked* him out. The ball glanced off the side of his head and bounded up into the stands.

"The next day I was handed a ticket to Portland, Oregon [home of the *Buckaroes*, a minor league team], by Mr. Lajoie, who insisted that all wild men belong in the West."

Most rookies to start in a losing cause

9 rookies
Houston Colt .45s   1963

The Colts fielded an all-rookie team against the New York Mets on September 27, 1963. But the new kids on the block got their blocks knocked off!

For one game at the end of the 1963 season, Houston manager Harry Craft fielded his greenhorn squad mainly as a novelty, hoping to reap a lot of publicity at Colt Stadium.

The average age of the Houston team was 19 years, four months. Outfielders Jimmy Wynn and Aaron Pointer were the only Colt starters old enough to vote at that time. Five of the starters had never played pro ball before the season began and three of them were starting for the first time in a major league game.

But the young squad, labeled "The Team of Tomorrow" by one newspaper, found it tough going in the here and now. The Mets crushed them, 10–3. Still, the youngsters managed to collect 11 hits and made only two errors. Before the game was over Craft used six more rookies for a total of 15.

Pitcher Jay Dahl, only 17 years old, was the youngest hurler to start a major league game since 1945. He lasted 2⅔ innings before he was yanked after giving up five runs. He was charged with the loss and never played in the majors again.

For the record, the Colts' all-rookie starting lineup included: Brock Davis, LF; Jimmy Wynn, CF, Aaron Pointer, RF; Rusty Staub, 1B; Joe Morgan, 2B; Glenn Vaughan, 3B; Sonny Jackson, SS; Jerry Grote, C; and Jay Dahl, P.

There's some question of how seriously the Mets took the frisky Colts. According to the *Houston Post*, "One Met asked another Met before the game. 'Are you starting against the Little Leaguers?' "

Most money lost by a rookie after *winning* a footrace with a teammate

$100
Miguel Dilone, Pittsburgh Pirates   1974

Speedy rookie Miguel Dilone saw easy money when slowpoke Willie Stargell challenged him to a footrace. But it was Stargell who ran off to the bank with the dough.

The cunning veteran threw down the gauntlet to the young speedster before a 1974 game, saying, "I'll race you from first to second base for a hundred bucks."

Dilone, knowing that Stargell would lose a race to his own shadow, readily agreed.

The rookie easily beat Willie by 50 feet. But when Stargell came plodding into second, he told Dilone, "Give me my money."

"What do you mean?" asked the puzzled rookie. "I won."

"I didn't say I'd *beat* you," Stargell replied. "I just said I'd *race* you for a hundred bucks!"

Dilone realized the slick veteran had just run a scam, not a race. Sadder but wiser, the rookie paid up.

Wildest debut inning pitched by a rookie

Bill Hoffman, Philadelphia Phillies   1939

The Phillies touted 21-year-old hurler Bill Hoffman as the new hometown hero. But his debut was so disastrous that he was quickly branded the new hometown zero.

Hoffman was pitching in a local industrial league when he caught the eye of Phillies owner Gerry Nugent. Desperate to improve a mediocre team that was catching hell from fans, Nugent signed the young hurler to a contract.

To his shock, Hoffman suddenly found himself plucked from obscurity and tossed into a major league game against the powerhouse New York Giants just two days later.

Recalled Hoffman, who entered the contest in the fifth inning with the Giants ahead, 7–0, "I was scared to death. The place was packed. And I'd never faced hitters like those guys in my life. I didn't know what to do."

When the frightened hurler began his first big-league inning ever, he unleashed three wild pitches, tying a record at the time. He also walked three batters and bounced a ball off Giants batter Zeke Bonura. New York scored three runs against the trembling newcomer before he retired the side.

Hoffman made brief appearances in just two more games before he was released and sent home for good.

Most people knocked out for calling a rookie "Mickey Mouse"

4 people
Cliff Melton, New York Giants   1936

When country boy pitcher Cliff Melton was trying to make the Giants' team in 1935, his floppy jug ears quickly earned him a humiliating nickname that nearly wrecked his big-league career. He was called "Mickey Mouse."

The moniker was tacked on during a spring training game when Gabby Hartnett of the Cubs yelled out, "Hey, Mickey Mouse, tie up those ears so I can see the infield!" Melton was so embarrassed he nearly crawled under the mound.

From then on, whenever someone shouted "Mickey Mouse," Melton couldn't pitch worth a hoot. His hurling suffered so badly that he was shipped back to the minors. But the nickname followed and his pitching suffered until he finally decided to take a stand.

When opposing manager Ray Schalk called him "Mickey Mouse," Melton charged into the dugout and knocked Schalk out cold. Anger wasn't the only thing behind Melton's punch. Melton just happened to stand 6 foot 6 and weighed 205 pounds.

Three times over the next few weeks, players called the hurler "Mickey Mouse." He flattened them all. After that, nobody dared use the nickname on him again.

Melton's pitching improved so dramatically that in 1937 he made the Giants—and won 20 games that season. Hatred of his nickname had turned Melton from a mouse into a man.

Shortest major league pitching career

1 warm-up pitch
Larry Yount, Houston Astros 1971

Hard-luck hurler Larry Yount finally experienced his lifelong dream. Unfortunately, it lasted just a few seconds.

Yount, older brother of Milwaukee Brewers All-Star Robin Yount, always wanted to play for the Houston Astros. And in 1971 he got the chance when the team called him up from the minors.

On September 15, the Astros were trailing the Atlanta Braves in the ninth inning when Yount was called on to make his major league pitching debut. The rookie bounded to the mound, thrilled beyond belief.

But on his very first warm-up toss, Yount injured his

right shoulder and couldn't go on. The crushed rookie went back to the bench, then back down to the minors—and never threw another ball in the bigs again.

Most embarrassing premature congratulations by a rookie

Jim Corsi, Oakland Athletics   1989

Young pitcher Jim Corsi learned a lot while playing for a minor league team in Tacoma, Washington. But one thing he didn't learn was how to count to nine.

Called up by Oakland in 1989, Corsi was thrilled beyond belief. In fact, during his first major league game, he was so excited that when A's pitcher Rick Honeycutt got the last out in the eighth inning, Corsi rushed out of the dugout to congratulate the hurler on winning the game!

Honeycutt stared at him and said, "They only play eight innings in Tacoma?"

The red-faced rookie slunk back to the bench. When Honeycutt got the final out an inning later, several Oakland players turned to Corsi and shouted: "Now, Jim, now!"

Most embarrassing "hat trick" by a rookie

Tim Layana, Cincinnati Reds   1990

When a hard shot hit by Cincinnati teammate Mariano Duncan rolled into the Reds' bullpen, rookie reliever Tim Layana scooped it up in his hat and playfully flipped it behind him into the stands.

Layana thought it was a foul ball. But the rookie turned as crimson as his cap when he learned it was fair—and that his stunt had cheated Duncan out of an extra base.

Duncan would have easily made it to third for a triple. Instead, the umpire called it a ground-rule double and made Duncan return to second in a 1990 game against the St. Louis Cardinals.

The next day, Layana took some serious razzing during pregame practice. St. Louis catcher Tom Pagnozzi pointed to the foul line and told Layana, "Now this side of third base is fair, and this side is foul." Cincy reliever Randy Myers told the rookie, "If you want more attention, just tell us. We'll mention your name."

A sheepish Layana told reporters later, "I remember filling out one of those player profiles when I was in the minors. One of the questions was, 'What was your most embarrassing moment?' I really didn't have one. But I do now!"

Longest delay in receiving the Rookie of the Year trophy

13 years
Pete Richert, Los Angeles Dodgers   1973

Dodgers relief pitcher Pete Richert had a so-so 3–3 won-loss record during the 1973 season, yet he received the Rookie of the Year award.

The trophy wasn't for his 1973 performance. It was for 1960—when Richert actually earned the trophy while playing in the minors for the Atlanta Crackers of the Southern Association, where he won 19 games and racked up 251 strikeouts in 225 innings.

The trophy mysteriously had vanished that year. In a flagrant delay of fame, the minor league president forgot that he had stashed it away in his basement and didn't find it again until he did some housecleaning 13 years later!

Managing to Look Foolish

WARPED RECORDS OF MANAGERS AND COACHES

Most oysters devoured by a manager in one pregame meal

100 oysters
Tommy Lasorda, Los Angeles Dodgers   1986

"If I can do it, you can do it," Dodgers manager Tommy Lasorda is famed for saying in his TV commercials for a weight-loss product.

Oh, yeah? Try doing what Tommy did during a 1986 road trip to Houston. He gobbled down a stupendous 100 oysters in one sitting during a pregame meal!

The hungry honcho went through three jars of horseradish in reaching the century mark in mollusk gluttony—and that was just for an appetizer!

Shortest term of a manager before resigning

18 hours
Eddie Stanky, Texas Rangers   1977

After accepting the job as manager of the Texas Rangers, Eddie Stanky didn't even last a full 24 hours before he shocked everyone by resigning.

Stanky, who hadn't piloted a team in nine years after managerial stints with the Chicago White Sox and St. Louis Cardinals, agreed to take over the reins of the Rangers on June 23, 1977. That day, his new team beat the Minnesota Twins, 10–8.

But after a sleepless night, Stanky realized he was a 60-year-old man whose family was more important than his job. So early the next morning he called Rangers executive vice president Eddie Robinson and said, "I quit."

Taking note of Stanky's brief stay, a Rangers fan told the *Dallas Morning News*, "Eddie would make an ideal mother-in-law."

Most roses thrown into the stands by a manager during a game

24 roses
Patsy Tebeau, Cleveland Spiders   1897

When his team blew a big lead against Baltimore on August 21, 1897, player-manager Patsy Tebeau saw red—and angrily showered the spectators with roses.

Tebeau had been tickled pink until the end of the fourth inning, because his Spiders were leading, 6–0. But between innings, friends of Cleveland's popular second baseman Cupid Childs presented the player with a big basket of 24 roses.

That didn't sit too well with the fiercely competitive Tebeau, who was playing first base that day. His mood only worsened when Baltimore exploded for six runs in the fifth inning to tie the score.

The first thing the fuming Tebeau saw when he returned to the bench was the basket of roses. "He picked up the big basket," the *Baltimore Sun* reported, "and hurled it with all his might into the grandstand, scattering the flowers in every direction.

"The peanut and chewing-gum vendors wore boutonnieres of roses the rest of the afternoon."

Most changes in the starting lineup made by a manager between games of a doubleheader

9 changes
Connie Mack, Philadelphia Athletics   1940

The A's rapped out 15 hits and scored eight runs in the first game of a doubleheader. Nevertheless, manager Connie Mack was so angry at his players that he benched all the starters for the nightcap and fielded an entirely new squad from leadoff man to pitcher.

The reason for Mack's fury between games of the 1940 twin bill was that the A's had been drubbed, 16–8, by the Boston Red Sox in the opener. Mack was so distressed that he wouldn't let Elmer Valo, Wally Moses, Dee Miles, or Hal Wagner start the second game, even though each player had banged out three hits in the first contest.

With the overhauled lineup, the A's did better in the

nightcap. They still lost—but this time, it was only by one run, 4–3.

Strangest dying words of a manager

George Stallings, Boston Braves   1929

George Stallings not only lived the game, he died the game.

In 1914, Stallings managed the Boston Braves when the team made baseball history. In last place on the Fourth of July, the club burst out of the cellar, climbed over every other team in the league, and won the pennant.

The team was forever known as "The Miracle Braves." And Stallings was called "The Miracle Man."

In his 13 years as a manager, Stallings lost a few more games than he won. And although he could accept defeat, he hated, more than anything, to lose a game because of walks.

In 1929, almost nine years after he last managed a team, Stallings lay on his deathbed. He opened his mouth to speak one final time. His wife moved closer . . . and with his last breath Stallings, a manager to the end, whispered: "Oh, those bases on balls."

Longest protest by a manager who knew he was wrong before he started to squawk

8 minutes
Earl Weaver, Baltimore Orioles   1978

Baltimore pitcher Mike Flanagan had just been called for a balk in a 1978 game against the New York

Yankees when cantankerous Orioles manager Earl Weaver came barreling out of the dugout to argue with the umpire.

"As Earl ran past me," Flanagan recalled, "he asked under his breath, 'Did you balk?' I said. 'Yes.'

"Nevertheless, he went over and gave [plate umpire] Tom Haller hell for eight minutes on how I didn't balk!"

Most managers used by one team in a game

4 managers
San Diego Padres   1984

During a beanball war that masqueraded as a baseball game, the San Diego Padres needed four managers. That's because the manager, the acting manager, and the acting acting manager were all ejected from the game. Fortunately, the acting acting acting manager kept his cool.

In the first inning of a 1984 game in Atlanta, Braves pitcher Pascual Perez drilled San Diego's Alan Wiggins with a fastball.

After that, Perez was a marked man every time he came to bat. He ducked out of the way of a high inside fastball in the second inning. Two frames later, Padres hurler Ed Whitson came close to knocking Perez's head off with a steamer. Manager Dick Williams was given the thumb for ordering the beanball.

Coach Ozzie Virgil replaced Williams. But Virgil was sent to the showers in the fifth inning after Padres pitcher Greg Booker again threw at Perez's head.

Coach Jack Krol took Virgil's place in the dugout. But in the eighth inning, San Diego hurler Craig Lefferts finally nailed Perez with a pitch—prompting a free-for-all between the teams and getting Krol booted out of the game.

The Padres were now piloted by Harry Dunlop, their fourth manager of the game. But the beanball war went on.

When San Diego's Graig Nettles was plunked by a pitch in the ninth, Braves skipper Joe Torre was ejected and replaced by one of his coaches. That meant a record total of six managers were used by both teams in the shameful game.

Biggest fine set by a manager for players *not* staying out late

$100
Gene Mauch, Philadelphia Phillies   1961

The 1961 Phillies were so inept they lost everything but their way to the ballpark. By late summer, baseball's biggest bumblers had piled up 19 losses in a row—and manager Gene Mauch was going bananas.

After trying everything to no avail, Mauch resorted to one of the zaniest major league moves ever. He imposed a reverse curfew on his team during a stay in Milwaukee.

"Gene told us, 'It's a $100 fine if I catch any of you in your room *before* 4:30 in the morning,'" recalled pitcher Jack Baldschun.

"So we all went out for nice long dinners or to the movies, and then to some bar. Only, the taverns closed around two. When I got back to the hotel, there was half the team in the lobby, trying to sleep!"

Incredibly, Mauch's wacky plan almost worked. Later that day his team was leading the Braves in the eighth inning. But Milwaukee tied the game and forced it into extra innings—and the pooped Phils ran out of steam, losing 7–6.

The Phillies didn't break their skein until they had dropped three more games for a total of 23 straight— the longest losing streak in modern baseball history.

Most games managed *after* getting fired

3 games
Don Zimmer, Texas Rangers 1982

Texas Rangers owner Eddie Chiles fired manager Don Zimmer—then promptly told him to manage the team's next three games until his replacement was found!

"Very strange," commented Zimmer.

"Shabby," said third baseman Buddy Bell.

Zimmer got the ax on July 25, 1982. Later that day Texas beat Milwaukee, 3–1, but the victory didn't sway Chiles as he continued to hunt for a new manager.

Over the next two days, the Rangers lost twice to the Brewers, 8–2 and 3–2. Then Zimmer's career at Texas came to an end when Darrell Johnson, a Rangers coach, was picked to replace him.

Ironically, six years earlier, Zimmer had replaced Johnson as manager of the Boston Red Sox.

As for the handling of Zimmer's Texas firing, Chiles admitted, "I think we came across looking inept."

Most cartwheels performed by a coach on one play

7 cartwheels
Arlie Latham, New York Giants   1909

Nineteenth-century star Arlie Latham racked up as many laughs as hits on the field. Baseball's first real comedian, the impish third baseman was so entertaining that he toured with a theater company in the off-season.

In 1909, Arlie became the third-base coach for the New York Giants. But show biz was still in his blood, so he humored the crowd by turning a few cartwheels down the third-base line whenever he waved in a run.

In one rousing performance during his first year in New York, the 49-year-old coach went feet-over-hands all the way from third base to home plate. He turned seven cartwheels in all, a head-spinning record that was still standing when they laid old Arlie to rest at age 92.

Most consecutive wins attributed to a manager's toupee

4 wins
Norm Sherry, California Angels   1977

Balding manager Norm Sherry popped on a hairpiece after he was hired to do ads for a toupee company—and, to his surprise, the Angels started a winning streak.

Whatever the reason, the team didn't come within a

hair of losing for four straight games. The manager and his team slowly became convinced the artificial surface atop his head was a good-luck charm.

That belief was reinforced when Sherry took the hairpiece off for repairs—and there was hell toupee. The Angels lost the next four games in a row!

Sherry quickly retrieved his magic rug. But then he faced a tough decision when his wife Mardie complained that she liked hubby's old chrome dome better. "She says the toupee makes me look like Howard Cosell," he told reporters.

The manager didn't have long to agonize over what to do. When the Angels kept losing, club brass flipped their wigs and fired Sherry.

Longest time a manager had his foot stuck in a garbage can

30 seconds
Pat Corrales, Texas Rangers   1980

Furious after a loss, Rangers skipper Pat Corrales vented his anger by kicking a plastic garbage can—but he booted it so hard that his shoe went right through it.

His players, who had expected to be trashed by Corrales, took one look at his weird footwear and doubled over in hysterics.

"It's hard to stand there with a garbage can on your foot," the manager recalled. "But what could I do? I was stuck. You can't hide something like that. It was so funny that we were all laughing."

Corrales got off easier than Atlanta Braves manager

Bobby Cox. While chewing out his team after a loss, Cox threw a clubhouse chair into the air—and it came down on his head, opening a bloody gash.

Said Cox, "I forgot what I was going to say, so I just walked away to get stitches."

Most *punts* by a manager in a game

3 punts
Gene Mauch, Montreal Expos   1969

Infuriated by an umpire's call, the Expos' fiery field boss Gene Mauch went on a wild kicking rampage that had spectators goggle-eyed with disbelief.

When a balk called by third-base ump Stan Landes let an Atlanta Braves runner score from third base to tie the game, 3–3, Mauch rushed out and argued the call at the top of his lungs.

After getting nowhere, the mad manager charged to the mound and punted the pitcher's resin bag 10 feet into the air. Then he ran after the bag and kicked it another 20 feet. Still not done, Mauch snatched the ball out of the hand of startled Expos pitcher Mike Wegener and punted it high into the air!

The next boot was of Mauch himself—right out of the game.

Worst managerial snub of a statesman

Eddie Stanky, Chicago White Sox   1967

Eddie Stanky lost a few Democratic fans when he gave Vice President Hubert Humphrey a headline-

112

making rebuff after the White Sox were whipped by the Minnesota Twins in a critical late-season game.

The steamed Stanky temporarily banned visitors from the Sox locker room so he could chew out his players in private. When a guard told him the Vice President of the United States was outside the door and would like to come in, Stanky stormed: "I don't care who it is. Nobody gets in here until I say so!"

The manager later claimed he didn't know the waiting visitor was the Vice President. But then he compounded the insult by snapping: "What do I need Humphrey for? He can't hit."

Only All-Star manager to lose in both leagues

Sparky Anderson, Cincinnati Reds   1971
Detroit Tigers   1985

Three men have managed both National League and American League teams in the All-Star Game, but just one has managed to lose on both sides of the fence: Sparky Anderson.

While helming the National League's Cincinnati Reds from 1970 to 1978, Anderson made four trips to the midsummer classic. He won three, but lost the 1971 contest, 6–4.

After switching to the Detroit Tigers of the American League in 1979, Anderson was named manager of the 1985 All-Star team. This time he lost, 6–1.

Alvin Dark and Dick Williams, the other two managers who've guided the All-Stars in both leagues, never lost while piloting National League teams.

So Anderson holds the dubious distinction of being the only double loser in All-Star Game history.

Wildest trashing of a dugout by an ejected manager

Chuck Cottier, Seattle Mariners   1985

Seattle skipper Chuck Cottier snapped when he was thrown out of a 1985 game for arguing a call—and he went on a crazed rampage that had a Yankee Stadium crowd of 50,000 gasping in disbelief.

Given the heave-ho for arguing over a checked swing, Cottier threw a fit . . . and then first base. He politely asked Yankees runner Dave Winfield to move off first base, then yanked the bag from its moorings and heaved it into right field. "People considered it a near-record toss in bag throwing," said a Mariners official.

Then Cottier stormed back to his dugout, grabbed three bats, and furiously flung them out onto the field one by one. Next, he snatched four helmets and spun them onto the diamond like Frisbees.

"Cottier trashed his dugout," said the official. "He threw the water cooler, gloves, shoes, whatever was there. He basically cleaned it out. Guys were running away so he wouldn't pick them up and throw *them* out on the field!"

When asked to assess Cottier's performance, Yankees manager Billy Martin, who was known to throw a temper tantrum or two, said, "I enjoyed it. On a scale of 1 to 10, I give it a 20."

Most first-base coaches used by a team in one inning

4 coaches
Washington Senators   1968

The Washington Senators had far less trouble getting runners on first base than keeping a first-base coach in a problem-plagued 1968 game.

Nellie Fox, the usual first-base coach, was ejected from the contest in the ninth inning. Second baseman Bernie Allen took over the post, but was needed to pinch-hit, so outfielder Cap Peterson replaced him.

But the umpire ruled that since Peterson had been previously announced as a pinch hitter and then replaced, he was technically out of the game, and couldn't coach first. So the Senators sent out pitcher Camilo Pascual—who became the team's fourth first-base coach that inning.

Quickest resignation by a manager at the start of a season

Opening Day
Eddie Sawyer, Philadelphia Phillies   1960

It took Eddie Sawyer just one game to realize his players were a bunch of world-class losers. After painfully watching the Cincinnati Reds paste his Phillies, 9–4, on the first day of the 1960 season, Sawyer knew his team was just as bad as it had been the previous year, when it finished in the cellar.

So he quit his job as manager on Opening Day.

Sawyer, who had managed in Philadelphia the two previous seasons, knew what he was doing. In 1960 the fizzling Phillies sported a pitiful 59–95 record, good for last in the league, a whopping 36 games out of first place.

Funny Business
WARPED RECORDS OF TRADES
AND CLUB EXECUTIVES

Biggest raise received after duping the owner
with a fake photo

$10,000
Babe Ruth, Boston Red Sox   1918

Can you picture potbellied Babe Ruth as a boxer? A clever sportswriter did—and pulled off a photo scam that landed Ruth a big salary increase.

The Bambino was griping one day to a friend, *Boston Herald* boxing editor Billy Hamilton, that he wasn't getting paid enough by Red Sox owner Harry Frazee even though Ruth was pulling in big crowds.

"So I told Babe, 'We'll make a fighter out of you just

to scare him,'" Hamilton recalled. "I got hold of a picture of Al Palzer, who was a heavyweight white hope, and I asked an artist in the office if he could put Babe's head on Palzer's body. He did a beautiful job.

"Then I wrote a story about how Babe Ruth was going to try his hand at boxing. The next day we printed the story and a photograph showing Babe in tights and a fighting pose.

"That afternoon Frazee called Babe into his office and asked him about the story. 'It's right,' said Babe. 'I've decided to try boxing because I'm not getting enough money in baseball.'"

Faced with losing his star player, Frazee immediately upped Ruth's salary $10,000 a year—a whopping amount in those days.

But Babe never would have made it as a boxer, Hamilton later confided to pals. "Just for the fun of it, we were sparring one day and I hit him with a punch in the belly that almost killed him!"

Longest distance an owner pushed a baseball with his nose

90 feet
Ted Turner, Atlanta Braves   1976

After buying the Braves in 1975, media mogul Ted Turner literally got down on his hands and knees to lure spectators out to the ballpark.

In an outrageous publicity stunt staged at Atlanta-Fulton County Stadium in 1976, Turner participated in "Field Day," when players engaged in wacky competitions before the game. Turner dropped on all fours and nudged a baseball from third base all the way to home plate as fans roared with laughter.

Turner proved even back then he had a nose for publicity.

Largest profit ever made after running a team into the ground

$63 million
George Argyros, Seattle Mariners   1981–1989

George Argyros was the luckiest owner in baseball.

Argyros bought the Seattle Mariners in 1981 for $13 million and wasted no time destroying the team. He traded away top players for lousy ones . . . paid the lowest salaries in baseball . . . lost some of his best players to free agency . . . and ruined the morale of the team.

He made Seattle the worst team of the 1980s. The Mariners were the only club that never had a winning season at home all decade. They usually finished so far out of first place that they would have needed a telescope to see the pennant. They rarely smelled victory; they just smelled.

Twice, the Mariners lost more than 100 games a year. Their overall record during Argyros's ownership was an ugly 673 wins, 893 losses.

But in spite of the incredible damage he had wrought, Argyros cut a deal in September 1989 to sell the Mariners to an Indianapolis group for $76 million. Amazingly, Argyros walked away with a profit of $63 million.

Largest check received by a player for meeting incentives that didn't exist

$20,000
Jim Winn, Chicago White Sox   1987

Reliever Jim Winn was thrilled when the White Sox front office cut him a $20,000 check for meeting certain incentives set by the club in 1987. The hurler was also shocked—because he had no incentive clauses in his contract.

Winn didn't even have a good year. He finished with 4 wins, 6 losses, 6 saves, and a sickly ERA of 4.79. In fact, his pitching was so mediocre that he was unceremoniously dumped by the Sox at season's end.

But even though they admitted it was a mistake, team honchos let Winn keep the money, giving him the incentive to say, "Thanks!"

Most Jell-O called for in a contract

37 boxes
Charlie Kerfeld, Houston Astros   1987

Money wasn't good enough for Astros relief pitcher Charlie Kerfeld when he negotiated a new one-year contract. He also demanded Jell-O!

And it wasn't until the Houston front office sweetened the deal with the quivery treat that Kerfeld inked the pact.

His wacky demand came after he learned fellow hurler Jim Deshaies had signed for $100,000. That sparked a bit of jell-osy on Kerfeld's part because he figured he was worth more than Deshaies. So he looked at his uniform number, 37, and asked for $110,037.37 plus 37 boxes of Jell-O.

"The front office went along with it just to placate Charlie," confided a teammate.

And what did Charlie do with the Jell-O? He used some of it for clubhouse pranks, like the orange Jell-O that was found in the whirlpool and in the toilets.

Most times traded or released by the same team

5 times
Bobo Newsom, Washington Senators   1937, 1942, 1943, 1947, 1952

The Washington Senators certainly would have understood if pitcher Bobo Newsom began chanting, "They love me, they love me not." They traded or released him *five* times!

After compiling a 31–31 record with Washington, he was traded to the Boston Red Sox in 1937. Five years later, after flings with the St. Louis Browns and Detroit Tigers, Bobo was sold back to the Senators for $40,000. However, after Newsom posted a disappointing 11–17 mark, Washington sold him to Brooklyn at a loss—for only $25,000.

Bobo was soon traded to the Browns again, who in turn sold him back to the Senators in 1943. There, he pitched for Washington in six games before packing his bags in a trade with the Philadelphia Athletics.

In 1946, he was once again pitching in the nation's capital. But midway through the 1947 season, the Senators dumped him again, this time to the New York Yankees, who released him at the end of the year. He appeared in 11 games for the New York Giants in 1948 and then was released.

Bobo tried a comeback in 1952 at the age of 44 with—who else?—the Senators. They treated him just like they did the other four times. They dumped him. Newsom and his 1–1 record were sent to the Philadelphia A's, where he ended his career at the age of 46.

Largest band hired by an owner to greet a player

100 musicians
George Steinbrenner, New York Yankees   1978

Relations between Yankees owner George Steinbrenner and pitcher Sparky Lyle hit a sour note during the 1977 season, and during the off-season, the pitcher still hadn't signed his new contract.

Sparky waited until spring training was underway before he decided to report to camp in Florida, still without a pact.

As he got off the plane in Fort Lauderdale, Sparky was shocked to find himself greeted by the 100-piece marching band from Hollywood Hills High School, complete with cheerleaders and pom-pom girls! The band carried a sign that read: WELCOME HOME, SPARKY LYLE—FINALLY.

Steinbrenner had hired the big band to try to patch up the sore spots between him and his hurler, who was one of baseball's best-known pranksters.

Sparky signed his contract. But after just one more season, the band-aid fell off—and Steinbrenner traded Sparky to the Texas Rangers.

Most players whom an owner put on waivers at the same time

25 players
Larry MacPhail, Brooklyn Dodgers   1941

Dodgers owner Larry MacPhail was so incensed that his team had lost the 1941 World Series that he obtained waivers on all 25 of his players in order to sell them to the St. Louis Browns.

After the New York Yankees crushed the Dodgers four games to one in the Series, MacPhail wanted to get rid of his entire team and gave the Browns—then one of the worst teams in baseball—the opportunity to buy all his players.

"We were waived out of the National League and sold to the Browns for $3 to $4 million," recalled Pete Reiser. "How did MacPhail get us out of the league? Master waiver.

"Everybody laughed and thought it was a joke. Time elapsed and we were waived—the whole club, lock, stock, and barrel. [Browns owner] Don Barnes started running around to the St. Louis banks to raise the money. 'What do you need the money for?' he was asked. 'I'm buying the Dodgers ball club for St. Louis,' he answered. They just thought he was crazy."

Fortunately for Brooklyn fans—and players—cooler heads prevailed. The deal was never made.

Most times a pitcher was let go by teams that went on to win the pennant

3 times
Big Jim Weaver, New York Yankees–Chicago Cubs–
Cincinnati Reds   1931, 1934, 1939

At 6 feet 7 inches, Big Jim Weaver was one of the tallest men ever to pitch in the major leagues. He also was one of the unluckiest. He was dropped by three teams just one year before they each won pennants.

Big Jim had been kicking around the minors for years when, at age 27, he was picked up by the Yankees in 1931. Although he had a 2–1 record, the team sent him back to the minors. Meanwhile, the Yankees won the flag the next year.

After Big Jim won 40 minor league games over the next two years, the Chicago Cubs acquired him in 1934. After compiling an 11–9 record, he was traded to the Pittsburgh Pirates. The next season the Cubs won the pennant.

The footloose hurler wound up with Cincinnati in 1938, but was released in the first month of the 1939 season—a year in which the Reds finished first.

And for the third time, Big Jim had to watch a former team play in the World Series without him.

Most players that an owner had tailed by detectives

25 players
Bob Carpenter, Philadelphia Phillies 1954

In a shameful episode of distrust, suspicious Phillies owner Bob Carpenter secretly hired private eyes to follow all 25 men on his club's roster to see what they were doing after dark.

Carpenter's spying came to light after Phils captain Granny Hamner noticed a car tailing him as he was driving home from a night game in Philadelphia. Worried about the mystery car, the infielder gunned the engine and roared through town—running red lights and screeching around corners with the other auto close behind.

After a wild chase, Hamner finally lost his tail. But he had barely arrived home when the car suddenly reappeared, circling the block. Hamner called the cops. They stopped the car and arrested the driver—who turned out to be a private eye toting a loaded revolver.

After Carpenter posted the gumshoe's $500 bond, the club owner confessed to newsmen he had been snooping on all his players. He claimed he did it just to make sure the guys didn't break curfew.

Fumed Hamner, "Gestapo tactics! If Carpenter wants to wreck his club, just let him go on treating all of us like two-year-olds."

Most teams on which a player belonged in the span of two days

4 teams
Gail Henley   1952

Depending on his point of view, outfielder Gail Henley could have felt very unwanted or very wanted. He went from one team to another four times within 48 hours.

Henley's amazing odyssey began October 13, 1952, when he was acquired by the New York Giants from a minor league team in Tulsa, Oklahoma. But before he'd even unpacked his bags, the Giants swapped him to the Cincinnati Reds for pitcher Frank Hiller.

Then, a day later, the Reds shipped Henley and two other players to the Pittsburgh Pirates in exchange for outfielder Gus Bell. In the span of 44 hours, Henley had been a member of one minor league team and three major league clubs.

Even worse, the Pirates then quickly sent him packing back to the minors. Not until two years later did Henley get to bat in the bigs. He played in 14 games for Pittsburgh before being shipped back to the minors for good.

Most money paid to an owner in exchange for his son-in-law

$225,000
Clark Griffith, Washington Senators   1934

Washington Senators owner Clark Griffith was not one who let his heart rule his head.

When the Boston Red Sox offered him $225,000 plus shortstop Lyn Lary for the Senators' All-Star player-manager Joe Cronin, Griffith agreed.

Except there was this one problem. The week before, Cronin had married Griffith's adopted daughter Mildred. In fact, Cronin was on his honeymoon through the entire period of negotiations and didn't have the slightest idea that his new father-in-law was peddling him.

The happy groom was steaming slowly through the Panama Canal on the last leg of his honeymoon when Griffith agreed to the deal on one condition—his son-in-law had to approve. Upon arriving at his hotel in San Francisco, Cronin was given the bombshell news.

He readily agreed to the deal. Besides receiving a lucrative contract, Cronin avoided an awkward situation. He knew that managers are hired to be fired. Having married the boss's daughter, Cronin said, it would have put a real strain on family relations if his father-in-law had to fire him.

Worst timing for offering pay cuts to players

Seattle Mariners   1987

After finishing last in the American League West in 1986, the Mariners brass felt the team could use a boost in self-esteem.

So the front office asked its players to show up for a seminar on positive thinking. After the players were in a good mood, management proceeded to ask several Mariners to take pay slashes of 10 to 20 percent!

Incredibly, team honchos wanted outfielder Phil Bradley to take a 10 percent salary cut even though he had batted over .300 for the previous three years.

The players began thinking positive, all right—they were positive they were working for a bunch of cheapskates.

Most consecutive years that a franchise changed managers

13 years
Kansas City–Oakland Athletics   1959–1971

Under the reign (of terror) of owner Charles O. Finley, the Athletics went through managers the way a slugger goes through bats.

Harry Craft (1) was fired after guiding his team to seventh place in 1959. He was replaced by Bob Elliott (2) who led the A's in a different direction—to eighth place in 1960. Finley then hired Joe Gordon (3), but fired him after only 60 games and replaced him with

Hank Bauer (4). Bauer finished that year and the next season with the A's in ninth place.

Finley then dumped Bauer and hired Ed Lopat (5), who managed the team throughout 1963, when K.C. finished eighth, and part of 1964 before he was canned and replaced by Mel McGaha (6). McGaha made it through the rest of the year and only 26 games into the 1965 season without getting the team out of the cellar before Finley fired him. New skipper Haywood Sullivan (7) didn't do any better.

The following year Alvin Dark (8) took over and guided the team to seventh place. But during the 1967 season, when the A's stumbled back into the cellar, Finley fired him and hired Luke Appling (9) to manage until the end of the year.

When the A's moved to Oakland in 1968, where they finished sixth, the new skipper was Bob Kennedy (10). He lasted a year before Finley replaced him with Hank Bauer (11) again in 1969. With the A's in second place in September, they underwent another managerial change. John McNamara (12) took over for the rest of the year and through 1970, when the team again finished second.

In 1971—the 13th consecutive year that the franchise was led by a different manager—Finley hired Dick Williams (13), who led the A's to the first of three straight pennants before quitting. Williams was the first skipper to finally work for Finley for at least two complete seasons.

Earliest curfew imposed on a team's PR man

9 P.M.
Harvey Greene, New York Yankees   1986

Fiery Yankees owner George Steinbrenner was furious at the team's public-relations director, Harvey Greene, during spring training in 1986.

Mean George called Greene's hotel room one evening and discovered the PR man had had the audacity to go out to dinner—at dinnertime!

Determined not to let such shocking behavior go unpunished, Steinbrenner ordered the culprit to be in his room by 9 P.M. every night for the rest of spring training.

"What's George going to do?" wondered one beat writer. "Make sure Harvey's by the phone in case George needs him to put a new spin on one of George's nightmares?"

Smallest gate receipts ever given a visiting team

$27.50
Boston Red Sox   1933

The Red Sox really got socked in the wallet when they played the St. Louis Browns on a rainy, bleak day in 1933. A mere 138 spectators showed up—one of the lowest attendance figures in modern major league history.

Before the game, Browns president Phil Ball was asked by his own front office to cancel the contest because of the lousy weather and lack of fans. "What do you mean, 'not play'?" Ball thundered. "I brought some friends as guests. I want to play the game!" So the teams played.

Boston's share of the gate receipts was a piddling $27.50, prompting the Red Sox's traveling secretary, Phil Tracy, to grumble, "That's not enough to cover the cost of the baseballs we used in batting practice."

From a fiscal standpoint, teams hated to play the Browns in St. Louis during the Depression era. The Browns were such a lousy club that few fans attended home games, so there was little profit for the visiting teams.

In 1935, for example, the Browns drew only 80,932 fans at home over the entire season—less than what many of today's teams draw in just one weekend!

Most times a player was traded even-up for the same player

2 times
Dick Coffman for Carl Fischer   1932
Wayne Nordhagen for Dick Davis   1982

The front offices of the St. Louis Browns and the Washington Senators acted like department stores with a very liberal return policy.

On June 9, 1932, the Browns sent right-handed pitcher Dick Coffman (5–3 at the time) to the Senators for left-handed hurler Carl Fischer (3–2). It was an even trade. Both sides suffered. Coffman went 1–6 for Washington while Fischer was barely better with a 3–7 mark for St. Louis.

Since that transaction didn't work out too well, the two teams made another deal—and so, on December 13th, they swapped back the same two players!

It was the first, but not the only, time that two major leaguers were traded even up for each other twice.

On June 15, 1982, the Toronto Blue Jays traded outfielder Wayne Nordhagen to the Philadelphia Phillies for outfielder Dick Davis. That same day, Philadelphia dealt Nordhagen to the Pittsburgh Pirates for outfielder Bill Robinson. But only one week later, Pittsburgh shipped Nordhagen back to his original team, the Blue Jays—in exchange for none other than Dick Davis!

Fastest cut from a team after a player's dog dumped a load in front of the coach's door

12 hours
Tug McGraw, New York Mets 1968

Hurler Tug McGraw got himself into deep doo-doo after taking his dog along to training camp.

The pitcher's dog, Pucci, put him in the doghouse the night before the final cut at the New York Mets' camp in St. Petersburg, Florida, in 1968.

McGraw opened his hotel room door to let in some air—and what happened next shouldn't happen to a dog.

"Pucci wandered out," McGraw recalled. "She trotted down the corridor to the room where [teammates] Dick Selma and Danny Frisella were living. They were having a party at the time . . . so they sort of boozed old Pucci up, feeding her a few nips.

"It must have upset her because she left a load right

in front of [coach] Joe Pignatano's room. Then Piggy came out of his room in his bare feet to see what the commotion was, and naturally he stepped smack into Pucci's deposit.

"Man, he put up a frightening clamor, complete with cussing and howling, the way only a coach can."

Just 12 hours later, McGraw was on his way to a Mets farm team in Jacksonville—accompanied by his hungover boozehound.

Biggest mortgage ever traded for a player

$300,000
Harry Frazee, Boston Red Sox owner   1920

When the New York Yankees acquired Babe Ruth from the Boston Red Sox, they received not only the most popular player in baseball but also a $300,000 mortgage on the Red Sox' home field.

The bizarre deal probably was illegal, but nobody questioned it because in those days trades were made fast and loose. Players in the minor leagues were swapped for mules, turkeys, and even oysters!

The Yankees officially paid $125,000 for Ruth's contract. But Yankees co-owner Jacob Ruppert also agreed to lend $300,000 to Red Sox owner Harry Frazee, who was fighting to stave off bankruptcy after he'd lost a fortune backing failed stage plays.

But Ruppert demanded security for his loan. So Frazee gave him a lien on his biggest asset: Fenway Park. The Yankees held the mortgage for five years. Then Frazee hit it big with the smash play *No, No, Nanette* and paid off the loan.

Today Babe Ruth remains the first and only player in baseball history ever to be traded for a mortgage on a big-league park.

Most players swapped in a major league trade

17 players
New York Yankees and Baltimore Orioles   1954

A massive trade between the Yankees and Orioles looked more like a cattle drive as nine players hoofed over to Baltimore and eight others were herded to New York.

That's a total of 17 players swapped, just one shy of fielding two complete baseball teams!

The deal was so big it was announced to the media in two stages. On November 18, 1954, Orioles general manager Paul Richards sent the club's two best pitchers, Bob Turley and Don Larsen, and starting shortstop Billy Hunter to the Yankees. In exchange, Yankees GM George Weiss shipped pitchers Harry Byrd and Jim McDonald, outfielder Gene Woodling, shortstop Willie Miranda, and minor leaguers Gus Triandos and Hal Smith to the O's.

Two weeks later, on December 1st, Baltimore sent pitcher Mike Blyzka, catcher Darrell Johnson, first baseman Dick Kryhoski, and outfielders Ted Del Guercio and Jim Fridley to New York in exchange for pitcher Bill Miller, second baseman Don Leppert, and third baseman Kal Segrist.

Despite the size of the trade, it did little to help either team. The Yankees, who finished second in 1954 with a 103–51 mark, won seven fewer games the year following the trade, although they did win the pennant. The Orioles finished seventh before the trade with a 54–100 mark, and the following year, they still ended up in the same position, having won only three more games.

Biggest pay raise given a player by a club president duped by a call-in radio show

$500,000
Chub Feeney, San Diego Padres   1988

As Padres president Chub Feeney was guesting on a San Diego radio talk show, a fan phoned in and said the salary of National League batting champion Tony Gwynn was far too low for such a fabulous player.

The fan suggested that Feeney rip up Gwynn's contract and give him a big raise. "Good idea," the president told the caller, and invited Gwynn's agent, John Boggs, to give him a call the next morning.

Boggs phoned right on schedule, and Feeney gave Gwynn a hefty $500,000-per-season pay hike.

Feeney didn't learn until later that the "fan" who had talked him into the deal on the radio was none other than Boggs's own secretary!

Most expensive congratulatory phone call ever made by an owner

$10,000
George Argyros, Seattle Mariners   1987

Mariners owner George Argyros buzzed San Diego Padres manager Larry Bowa long-distance to say "Well done!" after a Padres victory—and got slapped with a $10,000 fine.

That's because at the time he reached out and touched Bowa, Argyros was trying to sell the Mariners and buy the Padres. (The deal ultimately fell through.) Commissioner Peter Ueberroth had ordered the owner not to have any contact with San Diego personnel while negotiations were going on.

Unfortunately for Argyros, he couldn't have picked a worse time to call Bowa at the manager's office. While Argyros was gushing congratulations to Bowa for beating the Los Angeles Dodgers, who should be seated right across the desk from the Padres' manager? None other than National League president A. Bartlett Giamatti!

Most times traded between the same two teams within 8 months

3 times
Ron Hassey, New York Yankees–Chicago White Sox   1985–86

Catcher Ron Hassey felt like a Ping-Pong ball. He bounced from the New York Yankees to the Chicago

White Sox back to the Yankees and then back to the Sox—all within eight months.

Hassey's commutes began on December 12, 1985, when the Yanks swapped him and pitcher Joe Cowley to the White Sox for hurler Britt Burns, shortstop Mike Soper, and outfielder Glen Braxton.

But Hassey never even got a chance to put on a Sox uniform before he was shipped back to New York on February 13, 1986, in a seven-player deal that also saw the swift return of Braxton to Chicago.

Five months later, on July 30th, the two teams got into another trading frenzy—and when the dust had settled, Hassey found himself playing for the White Sox once more.

Hassey was no stranger to Chicago. He had played 19 games for the Cubs in 1984 before they shipped him off on his first tour of duty with the Yankees.

Most rap albums sold by a former team vice president

10 million albums
Stanley Burrell, aka M. C. Hammer, Oakland
Athletics   1990

Now M. C. Hammer he's got lots of bread/ But the man wasn't always so nicely fed/ Started out poor like you and me/ And he once even worked as the A's VP!

One day in the late 1970s, Athletics owner Charles O. Finley was entering the Oakland Coliseum when he spotted a kid named Stanley Burrell dancing for his supper. Finley offered the teen a job in the clubhouse, and he accepted.

Outgoing and likeable, Stanley soon was named an honorary vice president of the team. His title was more impressive than his salary, a mere $7.50 per game. The players nicknamed him Little Hammer because of his facial resemblance to Hammerin' Hank Aaron.

Eventually, Stanley talked former A's outfielders Mike Davis and Dwayne Murphy into giving him seed money for his own record label, Bustin' Records. Stanley changed his name to M. C. Hammer—and rapidly shot to stardom as a rap artist.

By the end of 1990, M. C. Hammer had sold more than 10 million albums. His second, *Please Hammer, Don't Hurt 'Em*, had sold more than 5 million copies alone. Charlie Finley was so impressed, he agreed to help his former VP. Finley went off to Europe to cut a deal to sell M. C. Hammer watches.

Said Hammer, "Charlie's workin' for me now."

The Bottom of the Barrel

WARPED RECORDS OF TEAMS

Most consecutive losses on a Thursday

16
New York Mets   1962–1963

In addition to being the worst team in modern baseball history, the first-year New York Mets also were victims of a bizarre phenomenon—"The Thursday Jinx."

For over a year, they simply couldn't win on a Thursday. True, they had difficulty winning on any day of the week. But for some strange reason, from the time the Mets came into existence, they lost 16 consecutive games played on a Thursday.

The jinx began on Thursday, April 19, 1962, when the Mets dropped a 9–4 decision to the St. Louis Cardinals. For the rest of the year, a Thursday game meant a Thursday loss—including twice getting swept in Thursday doubleheaders.

The jinx carried over into the first month of the 1963 season. Not until the 17th Thursday game in team history did the Mets finally break the weird streak. They beat the Chicago Cubs, 3–2, on a two-run homer by Frank Thomas.

Most runs scored by a losing team

23 runs
Philadelphia Phillies 1922

The Phillies racked up an amazing 23 runs against the Chicago Cubs on August 25, 1922—yet they still lost!

That's because the Phils were unlucky enough to unleash their hitting barrage on the day when their pitchers were still throwing batting practice—during the game. The Wrigley Field slugfest was the highest-scoring contest in major league history as the Cubs won, 26–23.

Chicago racked up 10 runs in the second inning alone, then added 14 more runs in the fourth frame. Cubs outfielder Marty Callaghan tied a major league record by batting three times in one inning. At the end of four frames, Chicago enjoyed a huge 25–6 lead.

But the Phils chipped away at the seemingly insurmountable margin and then exploded for eight runs in the eighth inning to cut the lead to 26–17. Philadelphia tallied another six runs in the final frame—and had the winning run at the plate—when their rally was killed.

Said Phillies third baseman Russ Wrightstone, "It's a crying shame that we wasted 23 good runs in one game. Heck, we don't score that many in a week."

Worst record in the final weeks of the season

1 win, 40 losses
Cleveland Spiders   1899

The Cleveland Spiders crawled into baseball history in 1899 by becoming certifiably the worst team ever to play in the major leagues.

These laughable losers piled up an amazing 134 losses against only 20 wins for the all-time lowest winning percentage of .130—and finished 84 games out of first!

The Spiders achieved this incredible mark of ignobility thanks to a flurry of losses at the end of the season unequaled in the annals of baseball. Of their last 41 games, the Spiders lost all but one!

On August 26th, the club embarked on a 24-game losing streak. Not until September 18th did they win again when they beat the Washington Senators in the opener of a twin bill. But the Spiders didn't even have time to enjoy the victory. They lost the nightcap, kicking off another losing skein of 16 straight games that ended only because the season was mercifully and finally over.

For Cleveland's last game ever (the club was disbanded after the season), the club was so desperate it recruited a cigar store clerk to pitch against the Cincinnati Reds. In true Spider fashion, he got smoked, losing, 19–3.

Most triple plays hit into in one game

2 triple plays
Boston Red Sox   1990

Until July 17, 1990, there had never been two triple plays in a single big-league game. But on that night at Fenway Park there were two—both hit into by the Boston Red Sox.

Each time, the Red Sox hit hard grounders to Minnesota Twins third baseman Gary Gaetti. Each time, Gaetti stepped on the bag and fired to second baseman Al Newman for the second out. Each time, Newman then threw to Kent Hrbek to get the runner at first.

Amazingly, Gaetti predicted the first triple play, which took place in the fourth inning. As Boston's Tom Brunansky stepped to the plate, Gaetti turned to Wade Boggs, who was perched on third, and said, "Have you ever seen a triple play? He's going to hit one right here."

Sure enough, Brunansky hit into the triple killing.

"Gaetti is a prophet, all right," Boggs later said. "I tip my hat to him and Nostradamus and Carnac the Magnificent. They're all peas in a pod."

Four innings later, Jody Reed hit into the game's record-setting second triple play. "Stick around," said Boggs. "We'll surprise you the rest of the year, too." The next night, the Red Sox and Twins hit into a total of 10 double plays—another major league record.

Most days between regular season wins

208 days
Baltimore Orioles   1987–88

Since the 162-game schedule was instituted in 1961, no team has gone as long between regular season wins as the Baltimore Orioles. After winning their final game of the 1987 season, the O's didn't record a victory for 208 days.

That's because the O-begone club set a major league mark by losing the first 21 games of the 1988 season.

In their third game, Baltimore lost again when pitcher Doug Sisk gave up a bases-loaded walk. The next day, the O's let the Cleveland Indians bat all the way around in two straight innings. In their seventh loss, Orioles batters got a mere two hits—both so weak they didn't even make it out of the infield. A dropped fly ball in the ninth inning allowed the winning run to score from first base in the O's ninth loss.

The comedy went on and on, with dropped balls, passed balls, misjudged balls, and errors galore adding more losses to the Orioles' pathetic record.

It wasn't until April 29, 1988—a whopping 208 days since the club's last regular-season win (on October 4)—that the Orioles finally managed a win, beating the Chicago White Sox, 9–0.

"We were ahead by nine runs in the ninth inning and I was still shaking," admitted Baltimore pitcher Dave Schmidt. "You never knew what was going to happen with us, the way it was going."

Most bases that a team deliberately let a runner steal in one inning

3 bases
Philadelphia Athletics   1915

The Athletics let Chicago White Sox hurler Urban "Red" Faber make the major league record book for a feat that he really didn't deserve.

In the fourth inning of a 1915 game in Chicago, the Sox had built a 4–0 lead when storm clouds built up and it began to rain. The A's, hoping for a rainout before the top of the fifth inning was completed, began to stall.

After Philadelphia pitcher Joe Bush hit Faber with a pitch, the A's infielders played back. Meanwhile, Faber, who wasn't exactly a gazelle on the basepaths, tried to speed up the inning by getting thrown out attempting to steal. However, the A's simply stood around like department store mannequins and let Faber swipe one base after another until he scored.

But the A's felt like real dummies when the expected cloudburst never came—and Faber's run proved to be the winning one in Chicago's 6–4 victory.

Most consecutive innings in which at least one batter was struck out

22 innings
Seattle Mariners   1986

Seattle batters went swishin' through much of 1986.

For 22 straight innings—from the seventh inning of April 27 to the second inning of May 1—at least one

Mariner walked up to the plate and sat right back down a strikeout victim.

The whiffs came during a shameful 17-game stretch in which the Mariners struck out a stupendous 180 times—an average of 10.6 per game. Within the span of five days, Oakland A's hurler Jose Rijo fanned 30 Seattle batters. Four days later, a record 20 Mariners were struck out by Boston Red Sox ace Roger Clemens.

Not surprisingly, Seattle set a new American League record for most strikeouts in a season with 1,148. That's like a team making every out a strikeout in more than 42 games!

Most consecutive defeats after staging a team parade

10 defeats
Atlanta Braves   1988

At the end of spring training in 1988, the Braves had high hopes of having their first winning season in four years. So they tossed a gala parade before Opening Day—and then went out and lost their first 10 games!

It was the worst start in National League history.

"The whole idea of the parade was to kick off what was supposed to be our big winning season," Braves public-relations director Jim Schultz ruefully recalled.

"We really hyped it. Just before the opener, [Braves owner] Ted Turner led the big parade down the middle of Atlanta. All the players and their families were riding in convertibles. There were brass bands and floats. The mayor and all the city dignitaries were out in force."

Then the Braves dropped the season opener . . . and

the next game . . . and the next . . . and the next. "We really kicked off the season—but the wrong way," said Schultz. "After our ten-game losing streak, we decided not to have another parade."

Last team that failed to hit a homer over the fence in its home park

Washington Senators   1945

Bleacherites didn't have to worry about getting conked on the head by a homer off a Senator's bat in 1945—because no one on the Washington club could swat a home run over the wall in its home park.

In fact, the team recorded only one round-tripper at Washington's Griffith Stadium all year—and that was an inside-the-park job by first baseman Joe Kuhel.

Griffith Stadium was just too cavernous for the slap-hitting Senators, who clubbed only 27 homers that season (compared to the 93 clouted by the league-leading New York Yankees). Griffith Stadium sported dimensions of 405 feet down the left-field line, 421 feet to straightaway center, and 320 down the right-field line.

The park was so spacious that outfielder Sam Rice played 19 seasons with the Senators without ever belting a fair ball into the stands at home.

Most pinch hitters used in a row without getting a hit

7 pinch hitters
Minnesota Twins   1979

Seven straight times, Twins manager Gene Mauch went to the bench. And seven times, his pinch hitters failed to get a hit.

It happened during a 1979 game against the Seattle Mariners. The Twins were losing, 6–4, in the seventh inning when Mariners right-handed reliever Byron McLaughlin took over for southpaw starter Rick Honeycutt.

Mauch, whose lineup consisted of right-handed batters, began using one left-handed pinch hitter after another.

First, he sent Ken Landreaux to bat for Dave Edwards, but Landreaux struck out. Then Hosken Powell hit for Willie Norwood, but he flied out. Next, Danny Goodwin went up for Jose Morales, but he also flied out.

Sticking to his strategic guns in the eighth inning, Mauch sent up Butch Wynegar for Glenn Borgmann. Wynegar popped out to the first baseman. Rob Wilfong batted for John Castino and drew a base on balls. Then Mike Cubbage, who was sent up for Bobby Randall, grounded out.

In the ninth inning, Glenn Adams—Minnesota's seventh straight pinch hitter—swung for Bombo Rivera and grounded to the first baseman, who booted the ball for an error. At that point, Mauch had no left-handed batters left except pitchers—and he wasn't crazy enough to use them.

In a pinch, the Twins fell short. They lost the game, 7–4.

Only team to fire a chimpanzee

Atlanta Braves   1975

Baseball fans went bananas when they learned the Braves had hired a chimpanzee to sweep off the bases at Atlanta-Fulton County Stadium after the fifth inning of each game.

For some reason, the silly plan triggered such a furious outrage that team bigwigs gave the monkey his pink slip before the 1975 season even started.

"There was such a hell of an uproar that we had to fire the monkey," recalled Bob Hope, the Braves' promotions director at the time. "The strange thing was that we never found out why people were upset. The animal lovers didn't seem to mind.

"We were trying to think of stunts that would attract people to the ball games. So we came up with the idea of training a chimpanzee and sending him out dressed like our grounds crew to sweep the bases and the players' and umpires' shoes.

"We weren't going to abuse the little monkey. We were just placing it in a role where the next step might be to sign it to a contract to play third base.

"But when the story hit the newspapers, it caused this terrible outrage from baseball traditionalists. Everybody was upset. So we fired the chimp."

Fewest runs scored in an inning on 3 walks, 5 stolen bases, 1 hit, and 1 error

1 run
New York Giants   1907

In the fifth inning of an April 27, 1907, game against the Boston Braves, the Giants collected one hit, drew three walks, stole five bases, and were gifted with an error.

Yet, despite all that frenzied activity, New York scored just *one* run!

Here's how they did it: The Giants' Sammy Strang led off with a single, the team's only hit in the inning. The next two batters popped out. With two down, Strang stole second and went to third on a throwing error. Cy Seymour walked and the two runners then pulled off a double steal as Strang scored from third.

After Roger Bresnahan walked, he and Seymour successfully attempted another double steal, the Giants' fourth and fifth stolen bases of the inning. With runners now on second and third, Dan McGann drew the third walk of the frame to load the bases. But the Giants came up short when Art Devlin ended the freaky inning by striking out.

Most errors gifted to a team that failed to score off any of them

8 errors
Chicago Cubs   1942

The Cubs were the beneficiaries of eight miscues by the Cincinnati Reds on April 19, 1942. But, incredibly,

Chicago failed to score a single run on any of the Cincy goofs and wound up losing the game.

Reds shortstop Eddie Joost committed four errors, third baseman Chuck Aleno flubbed three balls, and second baseman Lonny Frey was charged with one error. But not one of the miscues figured in the scoring.

The Cubs committed only one error, yet, ironically, it figured in their loss. Shortstop Lennie Merullo booted a ball in the ninth, allowing the Reds to tie the score at 1–1. Cincy went on to win the game, 2–1, in the 14th inning.

Wrote sportswriter Harold Winerip, "It would not have been considered improper if, after the game, the Cubs took to beating their fists against the wall and wailing that there just is no justice."

Most consecutive innings in which a team gave up at least one run

9 innings
Philadelphia Phillies   1923
Chicago Cubs   1964

The odds of a team's pitchers allowing the other club to score in every single inning of a game are a mind-boggling 1 in 451,834.

The 1923 Phillies and 1964 Cubs defied those odds.

On June 1, 1923, four Philadelphia pitchers gave up at least one run an inning against the New York Giants. The Giants exploded for four runs in the first, five runs in the fifth and sixth innings, and got at least one run in the other six innings. New York crushed Philadelphia, 22–8, and all but three of the runs were earned.

It looked as though the scoring streak would end in the ninth when Phils hurler Jim Bishop retired the first two batters. But then he gave up a triple and a double.

Forty-one years later, on September 13, 1964, five Cubs hurlers failed to pitch a shutout inning against the St. Louis Cardinals in a 14–2 drubbing.

The only St. Louis batter who failed to knock in a run was quintessential Hall of Shamer Bob Uecker.

A Fine Mess

WARPED RECORDS OF FINES AND EJECTIONS

Heftiest fine for hitting a home run

$100
Red Murray, New York Giants   1912

Giants outfielder Red Murray slapped a homer that won a game against the Pittsburgh Pirates—then got slapped with a stiff fine for doing it.

The odd situation developed when Murray stepped to the plate in the ninth inning with the game tied. Since there were no outs and New York had a runner on second, manager John McGraw naturally signaled for Red to bunt.

But Pirates pitcher Howie Camnitz whistled the ball

in high and inside. That just happened to be Murray's favorite "sweet spot"—and he instinctively swung with all his might, blasting the ball over the left-field fence.

Red romped around the bases and into the locker room, expecting congratulations for winning the game. Instead, McGraw stormed in behind him and fined the startled outfielder $100 for not bunting as he'd been told to do!

Most ejections in a month's time

5 ejections
Heinie Zimmerman, Chicago Cubs   1913

Heinie Zimmerman—the first National League player to win the Triple Crown in the 20th century — wielded a mean bat and an even meaner tongue.

His bat triggered hoorays; his tongue, heave-hos.

During one 30-day period in 1913, the Cubs' star third baseman was given the thumb five times. On May 19th, Heinie cussed out umpire Cy Rigler until the arbiter ejected him. On June 6th, he did the same thing to umpire Bill Byron and was tossed out of the game.

Exactly one week later, Zimmerman lambasted ump Malcolm Eason over a call at third base and, according to the *Chicago Tribune*, was "ordered out of the game quick as one could wink."

Two days passed before Zimmerman tore into another man in blue. After being called out at home, Heinie swore at plate umpire Bill Brennan, who promptly ejected him.

Two days later, it was umpire Bill Klem's turn to banish Zimmerman, this time for his obscenity-laced protest over a called strike—while he was perched as a runner on third base.

That ejection inspired a wealthy fan to intercede. The fan sent half of a $100 bill to Zimmerman and gave the other half to Klem. Heinie would get the second half only if he could avoid getting ejected for two weeks.

Zimmerman cooled it with the men in blue and won the C-note. But he still came out on the short end of the deal. Unable to swear at the umpires, he vented his anger at his manager, Johnny Evers. For a curse-filled screamfest at Evers, Heinie was fined $200.

Most expensive hair tonic worn by a player

$200
Casey Stengel, New York Giants   1922

Giants outfielder Casey Stengel "got the works" at the barber shop for two bucks. But he wound up getting clipped for a lot more than that by the end of the day.

Before a game with the Phillies in Philadelphia in 1922, Casey had a shampoo, haircut, and shave. Then his hair was neatly plastered down with a double dose of hair tonic.

Stengel looked and felt great when he showed up at the clubhouse. But then he noticed that manager John McGraw seemed to eye him with a slight air of disdain. Casey figured that McGraw was just having a bad day.

Within hours, Stengel was having one himself. During the game, Casey charged the mound after he was hit by a pitch from Lefty Weinert and triggered a brawl. After the umpires broke up the fight, they ejected Stengel.

"That was the silliest thing I ever saw on a ball field,"

roared McGraw. "But what can you expect from a sap who comes to the ballpark reeking of cheap gin!"

Stengel told reporters later, "There was no use trying to tell him that was not cheap gin but expensive hair tonic. He fined me $200. The fine stuck, too—just like the aroma."

Worst choice of a tune to sing to an umpire

"Three Blind Mice"
Bret Saberhagen, Kansas City Royals   1988

Disgusted with a call that went against his team, pitcher Bret Saberhagen turned his cap backwards on his head, put his hands over his eyes, and warbled "Three Blind Mice."

Saberhagen was sitting in the dugout at the time, but his mournful rendition reached the ears of plate umpire Nick Bremigan.

The song hit a sour note with the man in blue. He wasn't blind to Saberhagen's scorn and ejected the hurler with a nonmusical rendition of "Hit the Road, Jack."

Most days suspended for pitching with an emery board in the back pocket

10 days
Joe Niekro, Minnesota Twins   1987

There were three possible explanations why Twins pitcher Joe Niekro was carrying an emery board and sandpaper in his hip pocket when umpires confronted him during a 1987 game:

1. He planned to do his nails between pitches.
2. He was going to save a cosmetic surgeon's fee by giving himself a face-sanding.
3. He was doctoring the ball by scuffing it.

For some odd reason, league officials strongly suspected (3) and suspended Niekro for 10 days.

During his forced layoff, the hurler went on TV's "Late Night with David Letterman" to declare his innocence. When Letterman asked Niekro if he really was guilty of doctoring balls, the pitcher responded, "Do I look like a doctor?"

No, not a medical doctor. But he sure looked like a board-certified mound doctor. On the show, Niekro was wearing an apron with pockets that contained two bottles of Kiwi Scuff Magic, a pair of emery boards, a tube of Vaseline, sandpaper, scissors, tweezers, fingernail clippers, a clothes brush, and a nail file.

Oh, yeah. Niekro also was carrying a big power sander.

He was truly a man with the right scuff.

Only parrot ever to be ejected by an umpire

Pittsburgh Pirates "Parrot"   1987

It was a clear case of fowl play when a man-sized "parrot" launched a wacky attack on umpire Fred Brocklander during a Pirates-Dodgers game in Pittsburgh in 1987.

Pirates mascot Tom Mosser, costumed as a parrot,

targeted Brocklander after the umpire made a call that went against Mosser's beloved Bucs in the fifth inning.

The ump ruled that Pirates right fielder Andy Van Slyke had trapped a sinking liner while attempting a diving catch. TV replays on the electronic scoreboard seemed to show otherwise. Moments later, the Dodgers' Pedro Guerrero slammed a three-run homer in Los Angeles' 10–2 victory.

After the homer, the Parrot hopped on his three-wheeled motor scooter, chugged straight toward Brocklander, and, to the delight of the fans, threw a Nerf ball at him.

The furious ump thumbed birdman Mosser out of the game. The Parrot then lit out on his scooter for the safety of the center-field fence. After the game, Mosser was read the riot act by the umpires and the next day, the league clipped the Parrot's wings and suspended him for one game.

Biggest fine assessed a coach for having a birthday

$50
Bing Miller, Chicago White Sox   1944

White Sox coach Bing Miller had a "fine" time on his 50th birthday. Instead of the usual ho-hum tie or socks, Chicago manager Jimmy Dykes presented him with a $50 fine.

Miller hit the half-century mark in Detroit on August 30, 1944. His team gave him an early gift by destroying the Tigers with a 15-hit performance. Then, that evening, Miller waltzed off to attend a birthday party tossed for him by some Detroit friends.

The bash ran late, so he stayed overnight at his pals' home. When Miller returned to the team's hotel the next morning, Dykes was the first person he ran into.

"Nice morning, isn't it?" Miller said pleasantly.

"That's going to cost you 50 bucks," Dykes snapped.

Miller was stunned. "You mean you're fining me $50 for saying it's a nice morning?"

"No—for being out all night without telling me where you were going," replied Dykes. "The rule goes for you just like everybody else on the club."

Miller walked away in a daze, mumbling, "Fifty dollars for celebrating my 50th birthday. It's a good thing I'm not a hundred years old!"

Most players ejected by an imposter

4 players
Jim Colborn, Milwaukee Brewers   1976

Brewers pitcher Jim Colburn threw his own team a curve at the close of the 1976 season. The prankish pitcher disguised himself as an umpire and thumbed four teammates out of the game before it even began.

Garbed in a borrowed outfit, complete with a chest protector and a mask that hid his face, Colborn joined the umpires and managers at home plate for the exchange of the lineup cards.

Although the real umps were in on the gag, neither Milwaukee manager Alex Grammas nor Detroit boss Ralph Houk recognized Colborn at first. "Then I said, 'Have a nice winter, Alex,' " recalled the hurler. "He gave me a glance, went back to talking to Ralph, then did a great double take and yelled, 'What the hell are *you* doing out here?' "

After a few laughs, Colborn immediately strutted over to the Brewers' dugout and ejected four players. "I did it as a favor," he later claimed. "Since it was the last game of the season, they wanted to go home early. But the ejections didn't stick. I tried to throw myself out, too, but it didn't work either."

Stiffest fine for striking out a batter

$50
Jim Walkup, St. Louis Browns   1935

Most pitchers are happy when they strike out a batter. But when hurler Jim Walkup did it during a 1935 game, he was horrified!

That's because Walkup knew he had just violated an ironclad rule of hard-nosed Browns manager Rogers Hornsby, who decreed that on an 0-and-2 count, his pitchers must waste an outside pitch—or else be fined $50.

Fifty bucks was a lot of money during the Depression. So when Walkup ran an 0-and-2 count, he carefully threw the next pitch outside the strike zone. But to his shock, the umpire thought it had nicked the corner and yelled, "Strike three!"

Spectators' jaws dropped as Walkup raced to the plate and desperately argued over the call, begging the umpire to reverse it.

"I went running in halfway to home plate, yelling, 'No! No! That was a ball!' " Walkup recalled. "The ump looked at me like I was crazy. 'Whose side are you on?' he asked me."

The ump stood firm—and so did Hornsby when he fined Walkup 50 smackers.

Fewest pitches thrown before getting ejected

1 pitch
Bob Babcock, Texas Rangers   1980

Reliever Bob Babcock's first mound appearance as a Ranger ended fast when he was tossed out of the game after just one pitch—for throwing a beanball that missed!

The young hurler had the misfortune of being used as cannon fodder in a beanball war between Texas and the California Angels. Tensions mounted when both teams engaged in a bench-clearing brawl in the sixth inning.

In the top of the seventh, Babcock, who was making his first appearance of the season after being called up from the minors, was summoned to the mound. Rangers manager Pat Corrales handed him the ball and gave him orders on how to pitch to the next Angels batter: Hit the SOB!

"That happened to be Dan Ford," Babcock said. "As I went into my windup, Ford ran out of the batter's box and I missed him. He was already moving when I threw the ball. It sailed behind where his head had just been and went to the backstop. He didn't want to get hit and I didn't blame him. He knew it was coming."

The umpire immediately thumbed Babcock out of the game. The pitcher tried to play dumb. "I told him my foot had slipped off the rubber, but the umpire wouldn't buy it. He just told me, 'Get outta here!'

"What makes me mad is that I got charged with a wild pitch. Hell, I would have nailed the guy dead center if he'd stood still!"

Earliest ejection of a catcher

10 minutes before *the game*
Al Lopez, Brooklyn Dodgers   1934

Al Lopez used a photo to prove foul-tempered umpire Bill Klem had blown a big call. But when the ump got the picture, the catcher got the thumb.

As a result, Lopez was in the showers 10 minutes before the game even started!

The disputed call came in a 1934 contest as the Dodgers' catcher tried to tag out a runner at home. "I knew I had the plate blocked, but Klem called the guy safe," Lopez recalled. "I came off the ground yelling my head off. Klem wouldn't listen. He just indicated the runner had slid in under the tag."

But the next morning, much to Lopez's delight, a newspaper published a picture of that very play—which clearly showed the catcher had made the tag.

That afternoon, Klem strode to home plate to start the day's game and noticed the plate was covered with dirt. He took out his whisk broom, brushed it off—and found himself staring at the newspaper photo taped to the plate.

Klem furiously ripped the picture off the plate, thrust it under Lopez's nose, and bellowed: "Yer outta here!"

For Lopez, there was no Klemency.

Longest time between angering an umpire and getting ejected

4 years
Jeff Tesreau, New York Giants   1914–1918

Crochety umpire Bill Klem nursed a grudge against a player for four long years before exacting revenge.

Klem detested his nickname, "Catfish," so naturally players teased him about it at every opportunity—which always brought a swift ejection whenever he caught them saying it.

During a 1914 game, New York pitcher Jeff Tesreau hid near the Giants' bench and began yelling, "Catfish! Catfish!" Klem went crazy and started booting Giant after Giant out of the game. But still the taunts went on.

Days later, Klem learned that his tormentor was Tesreau, but the ump did nothing about it for four years.

Then, during a 1918 game, someone on the Giants' bench yelled, "Catfish!" Klem turned purple and looked for Tesreau in the dugout. But the hurler was far away in the bullpen.

Nevertheless, the ump stalked to the bullpen, gave Tesreau the thumb, and bellowed, "Go to the clubhouse—and that'll cost you 25 dollars besides!"

"What for?" sputtered the stunned pitcher.

Klem retorted, "For 1914, *that's* what for."

Most players on one team ejected in a game

15 players
Brooklyn Dodgers   1951

They called it "The Boston Beef Party."

During a late-season game with the Boston Braves in 1951, the Brooklyn Dodgers put up such a beef with the umpire over a call that 15 of them were given the thumb.

The Dodgers, desperately trying to hold on to first place in the final week of the season, were deadlocked, 3–3, with the Braves in Boston in the bottom of the eighth. Then came the critical play of the game.

Umpire Frank Dascoli called the Braves' Bob Addis safe on a bang-bang play at the plate. Dodgers catcher Roy Campanella was outraged. He threw down his glove, wheeled around, and spewed a few choice words at the ump.

In a flash, Dascoli thumbed Campy out of the game. Then the catcher's teammates took up his fight with a verbal assault on the umpire. One by one, Dascoli ejected the Dodgers until there was no one left on the bench. The final toll: 15 players banished.

After the game, which the Dodgers lost, 4–3, Dascoli had to be protected by a cordon of police as enraged Dodger Jackie Robinson tried to batter down the door of the umpires' dressing room. (He was fined $100 the next day by league president Ford Frick.)

The mass ejection was the largest in major league history, topping the old mark of 14 Chicago White Sox who were given the thumb by umpire Red Jones in a 1947 game with the Boston Red Sox. As they left the field, Sox coach Bing Miller held up his glasses and told Jones, "Here, take these. You need 'em more than I do."

Longest time it took a player to leave the game after being ejected

10 minutes
Casey Stengel, Boston Braves   1924

The cops had to be called to haul away hotheaded Casey Stengel after he was thumbed out of a 1924 game and refused to leave.

The legendary baseball oddball was ejected by umpire Jack Powell after furiously protesting a called strike. But instead of trotting off to the showers, Casey trotted right back to his outfield position after the Braves were retired.

When he reached his post, Casey stripped off his shirt and threw it on the ground.

"I did it," he later explained, "because I was so hot over that fellow's decision that I had to cool off."

Powell spotted the barechested player and promptly got the cops on stadium duty to escort Casey not only off the field, but completely out of the stadium.

Only coach ever to get ejected for eating popcorn

Germany Schaefer, Washington Senators   1912

Player-coach Germany Schaefer liked to irritate other teams by munching on popcorn in the coach's box during games. He wanted to show just how little he regarded them.

But when Schaefer appeared in the first-base coach's box with his bag of popcorn during a 1912 game with the Chicago White Sox, umpire Silk O'Loughlin showed just how little he regarded Germany.

The fed-up ump booted Schaefer out of the game on the grounds he was hurting the dignity of the national pastime. So Schaefer bagged himself a record—becoming the only coach ever given the thumb for eating popcorn.

Most expensive pregame toss

$275
Duke Snider, Los Angeles Dodgers   1958

Strong-armed outfielder Duke Snider bet a teammate he could throw a baseball out of the expansive Los Angeles Coliseum. But he injured his arm in the attempt and was fined for being unable to play.

Just before a game against the Chicago Cubs on April 23, 1958, Snider and his Dodger teammate Don Zimmer got into a contest to see who could hurl a ball over the Coliseum's rim. It was no easy feat. The rim was 79 rows up and 106 feet high.

With $400 in side bets lined up, Snider hurled his first ball and came up short by only a few feet, to the 76th row. He wound up and threw again with all his might—and that's when the Duke overextended his right elbow and it went *pop*!

Snider then confessed to Dodgers manager Walt Alston that he was in too much pain to play. Furious, Alston fined him one day's pay—$275—for his horseplay and sent him home. Although Zimmer didn't hurt himself, he was fined $25.

Faced with a $275-a-day fine for every game he missed, the Duke made a quick recovery and was back in the lineup the very next day.

Most games in which a player carried a rule book in his back pocket

1,572 games
Ivy Olson, Cleveland Indians–Cincinnati Reds–
Brooklyn Dodgers   1911–1924

Scrappy infielder Ivy Olson loved nothing better than a good argument with an umpire—and to prove his point in disputes, he always lugged a rule book in his back pocket.

Ivy made umpires break out in a rash. At the screaming height of a squabble, he'd yank out his book and start flipping through the pages with an exaggerated flourish. But Ivy rarely had time to find the appropriate rule before the apoplectic ump thumbed him out of the game.

Ivy, whom arbiters nicknamed "Ivan the Terrible," carried his trusty rule book in every game for 14 years.

Biggest fine for throwing bread at the manager

$100
Christy Mathewson, New York Giants   1912

Giants pitching great Christy Mathewson once fired a fast-breaking bun at the head of his manager, John McGraw—and it cost the hurler a wad of dough.

While the Giants were in the dining car of a train bound for Boston, several players pulled the soft dough out of their buns and began playfully tossing it at McGraw. But they all missed. So Christy boasted, "Let a sharpshooter show you how." Then he let fly with an entire hard bun.

The bread missed McGraw but hit his female dinner companion in the back of the neck. The manager turned around, but said nothing. However, when Christy picked up his paycheck the next day, he found it was $100 short—with a note saying he had been fined.

Christy confronted McGraw and asked, "Do you mean you're fining me $100 simply for hitting a woman with a bun?"

"You aimed at me, didn't you?" McGraw asked.

"Sure I did," the pitcher admitted.

"You're supposed to have the best control of any pitcher in the league," said the manager. "Last night, you proved to be a bad example to our young pitchers. I fined you $100 for poor control!"

The fishiest ejection ever given by an umpire

Bill Summers, American League 1947

Plate umpire Bill Summers fielded a fish during a game between the visiting St. Louis Browns and the Boston Red Sox at Fenway Park.

Browns hurler Ellis Kinder was starting his windup when Summers noticed a small silvery object land behind the pitching mound. Instinctively, the umpire called time and hustled out to investigate. There on the ground was a dead fish.

First, Summers looked into the stands to see if a fan had hurled the fish onto the field. No one had. Then he looked up and spotted the culprit—a sea gull! It had been flying overhead when it involuntarily dropped the fish it was carrying after getting attacked by other hungry gulls.

As the birds watched from above, Summers picked up the finny food by the tail and carried it at arm's length to a groundskeeper for a proper burial. Summers then rubbed his hands in the dirt to get rid of the fishy smell.

As he returned to his position behind the plate, the crowd gave the umpire a big ovation—and that's no fish story.

The *Fanimal* Kingdom

WARPED RECORDS OF FANS

**Most days a fan sat atop a flagpole
waiting for his team to win a pennant**

*117 days
Charley Lupica, Cleveland   1949*

Daffy druggist Charley Lupica climbed onto a platform at the top of a 20-foot flagpole on May 31, 1949. He boldly announced that he'd stay there until his beloved Cleveland Indians—world champions the year before—won the American League pennant again.

Fans questioned his sanity considering the fact that the Indians were in seventh place at the time Charley began his flagpole vigil. And the way they were playing, it looked like they were going to end up in the cellar and leave their biggest fan up in the air.

But Charley was still high on his Indians. So he kept sitting and sitting on his four-foot-square platform through wind, rain, and blazing summer heat.

Finally, on September 25th, 117 days after his ordeal began, Charley stiffly crawled back down to earth.

By then it was obvious the Indians weren't going to win the pennant. But at least they had moved up to fourth place.

However, all was not lost. Indians owner Bill Veeck was so impressed with Charley's loyalty that he gifted the diehard fan with a new car.

Shortest time in which a fan botched catching two foul balls

30 seconds
Ron Vachon, Fenway Park, Boston   1990

Most big-league fans never get a chance to catch a foul ball. But Boston Red Sox rooter Ron Vachon had two chances in the span of half a minute—and blew them both.

During a game with the Oakland Athletics at Fenway Park on September 4, 1990, the A's Rickey Henderson fouled a pitch that hit off a luxury box behind Vachon's seat. The ball ricocheted right to Vachon. He reached for the ball, but it bounced off his wrist to the seats below. The crowd booed.

Vachon glumly sat down, cursing the muff. But just 30 seconds later, Henderson fouled another pitch to the roof of a luxury box and it glanced back to the same fan again. Incredibly, Vachon dropped that ball, too! Again, the crowd booed.

"The first one was tough, but I blew it on the second one," recalled Vachon, a bank employee. "I couldn't believe I'd have another chance. I just stood there and bobbled it."

Added Vachon, who left the game red-faced and empty-handed, "I haven't caught a ball since I was 13."

Most cucumbers thrown at an umpire

100 (est.)
Sportsman's Park, St. Louis   1915

An umpire really found himself in a pickle when he enraged the crowd during a St. Louis Cardinals game and suddenly found himself being pelted by, of all things, cucumbers!

The bizarre vegetable barrage came in the ninth inning of a 1915 game with the Chicago Cubs at Sportsman's Park in St. Louis. Umpire Bill Byron called Cards runner Art Butler out, then booted him from the game when the player put up an argument.

Suddenly cucumbers came flying down at the umpire from every section of the bleachers and stands. When the veggie shower ended some 100 cucumbers later, the startled arbiter found himself standing in the middle of what looked like a giant green salad.

To this day, one of baseball's biggest mysteries still remains: Why did all those fans come to the ballpark with cucumbers?

Greatest number of fans to change seats simultaneously during a game

3,000 fans
Crosley Field, Cincinnati   1942

The Cincinnati Reds were leading the visiting New York Giants, 2–1, in the fifth inning when suddenly 3,000 Crosley Field spectators on the first-base side of the grandstand got up and moved en masse across to the third-base side.

And they stayed there for the duration of the night game, which was played on August 25, 1942.

The big move followed an announcement on the public-address system that an eclipse of the moon was due to begin within minutes, and could be seen more clearly from the left side of the ballpark. Since there were plenty of empty seats, most of those fans with seats on the first-base side made the switch.

The Reds won the game, 3–1, prompting one waggish New York sportswriter to report that although the moon's eclipse could be seen from only one side of the ballpark, "the Giants' eclipse could be seen from any seat in the park."

Grossest fan's welcome ever received by a pitcher

Dave Smith, Houston Astros   1986

Houston Astros relief ace Dave Smith was used to getting showered with adulation by fans. But during a 1986 visit to New York's Shea Stadium, he got a golden shower—when a Mets fan "welcomed" the hurler by peeing on him!

Smith was sitting in the bullpen when he felt something spraying down on his head. To his shock he discovered that a beer-guzzling bozo in the bleachers above the bullpen was performing his own version of tinkle, tinkle on a star.

After Smith's wet welcome to the Pee Wee Wee League, he quipped: "It's the first time I've ever been used for long relief."

Most fans who carried a rabbit's foot to hex an opposing pitcher

40,000 fans
Municipal Stadium, Cleveland   1951

Nobody scalped the Cleveland Indians better than New York Yankees pitcher "Steady Eddie" Lopat. By 1951, the hurler had beaten Cleveland 11 games in a row.

So, in a desperate attempt to change Lopat's luck and stop his streak, Cleveland fans tried to cast a bad-luck spell on him.

Surprisingly, it worked!

When New York visited Cleveland for a night game on July 14th, the first 40,000 Indians fans who showed up were given a rabbit's foot by the club's management.

One fan employed a wilder tactic to try to hex the hot hurler, Lopat recalled. "While I was warming up before the game, a drunk came on the field and threw a black cat at me, and it clung to my jersey."

The mass whammy was just too much for Lopat. That old black magic had him in its spell, and he lost the game, 8–0.

But after that game, "Steady Eddie" went right back to winning, eventually racking up a career record of 40 wins and 12 losses against the Indians.

Most years a fan blew up balloons in honor of a player

6 years
"Fierce" Jack Pierce, Ebbets Field, Brooklyn
1937–1942

Cheering for his baseball hero wasn't enough for Jack Pierce. He put on a blowhard tribute that included bursting balloons every time his idol came to the plate.

As far as Pierce was concerned, Dodgers third baseman Cookie Lavagetto was the greatest player who ever lived. So beginning in 1937, when Cookie first joined the team, Pierce attended nearly every home game and performed the same wacky ritual each time.

He always bought 10 box seats just behind the visitors' dugout so he had plenty of room. Then Pierce spread out a large blue-and-gray banner bearing the name COOKIE on top of the dugout.

Next, he began furiously inflating a gross of "Cookie" balloons with a hand bellows—screaming his hero's name over and over as he worked. As each balloon neared the bursting point, he'd yell one last "Cooooo-keeeee!" and then pop the balloon. Pierce also had a dozen helium-filled "Cookie" balloons delivered by cab to his seat at Ebbets Field. Whenever Cookie got a hit, Pierce would send up one of these special balloons.

Pierce's dazzling display cost him $40 to $50 a game, a lot of loot back then. Fortunately, he owned a prosperous Brooklyn restaurant and could afford it.

Although Lavagetto went off to war after the 1941 season, Pierce continued his weird tribute for another year before his obsession with Cookie crumbled.

Largest number of fans who lied to get into a game free

14,000 fans
Hilltop Park, New York   1905

When a game between the visiting Washington Senators and the New York Yankees was rained out in the fifth inning, club officials had a problem. Back then, rain checks were printed separately from admission tickets. The club was out of rain checks, so management told the Hilltop Park crowd of 6,000 to just show up at the gate the next day for free admission to the makeup game.

When the gates opened the following afternoon, 20,000 fans were waiting outside—all claiming they had been to the game the day before!

Since officials had no way to check on who was lying, they had to give free admission to the whole crowd—including the 14,000 liars.

Most runs scored against a team after its fans tried to mentally will a victory

13 runs
Baltimore Orioles   1988

During their record-shattering, season-opening 21-game losing streak in 1988, the Baltimore Orioles received psychic relief from their fans.

After the 15th straight O's defeat, famed mentalist the Amazing Kreskin got on the radio and asked Orioles fans to join him in beaming positive thoughts to the team moments before it played the Royals in Kansas City.

"Just concentrate your mental powers," Kreskin told rapt listeners. "Thaaatt's it . . . just concentrate . . . and remember . . . think positive thoughts. . . ."

The Orioles took the field, their brains brimming with positive thoughts—and then gave up nine runs in the first inning. Baltimore starter Mike Morgan lasted only 12 minutes and didn't get a single batter out. When the slaughter ended, the Orioles had lost their 16th straight, this time by a score of 13–1.

Apparently the fans sent their brain waves to the wrong clubhouse.

Only fan ever to lose out by being first in line for tickets

Robert Hunt, St. Louis   1964

After his beloved Cardinals won the 1964 pennant, St. Louis fanatic Robert Hunt rushed to the ballpark days in advance so he could be first in line to buy World Series tickets. But his devotion cost him a bundle.

He got his tickets, all right. But when his boss saw Hunt's picture splashed in the newspapers as an early-bird ticket buyer, Hunt got fired for skipping work.

A bill collector who had been looking for Hunt also spotted his photo and nabbed him. Then Hunt got arrested for nonsupport of his family.

After the Series, Hunt was first in line again—this time at the unemployment office.

Most fans helped out of the ballpark for laughing too hard

4 fans
Comiskey Park, Chicago   1923

Babe Ruth and a puppy put on such a hilarious show at Comiskey Park that four fans needed to be assisted from the stadium because they were laughing so hard.

The New York Yankees were cruising to an easy victory over the Chicago White Sox in the bottom of the ninth inning when a puppy wandered out to left field, where Babe was playing. Bored with the game, Ruth got down on his hands and knees and started following the dog around. The fans loved it.

Ruth then tossed his glove at the li'l doggie to scare it off the field. Instead, the puppy grabbed the mitt in its mouth and ran away. As portly Babe rambled after the pooch, the crowd exploded in laughter. The funny spectacle was still going on when suddenly—*craaack!*—batter Paul Castner walloped a fly ball right to the spot where the gloveless Ruth and the mongrel were romping.

Without even breaking stride in his chase, Babe reached out and nonchalantly caught the ball bare-handed!

The fans went nuts and laughed themselves silly. Reported Paul Gallico of the *New York Daily News*: "Four strong men were assisted from the park in hysterics."

Most muggers beaten up at one time by a future Hall of Famer

3 muggers
Ty Cobb, Detroit Tigers   1912

A trio of muggers got more than they bargained for when they attacked tough Ty Cobb as he was driving to the Detroit train station late one night.

Although Cobb was in a hurry to make the train, he pulled over when three men signaled for help. But then they quickly hopped on the running board of Cobb's Chalmers and started punching him through the open window. Cobb slid across the seat, leaped out through the passenger door—and charged the thugs.

One mugger went down in a flurry of fists. A second mugger slashed Cobb on the back with a knife, but the Detroit star, who was carrying a big Belgian-made revolver, pistol-whipped the slasher.

All three thieves then ran for their lives with Cobb in hot pursuit. He trapped the third mugger in an alley and beat him unconscious with his pistol.

Cobb then boarded the train just as it was pulling out. Not until a teammate noticed blood soaking through the back of the star's coat did Cobb get his knife wound treated and bandaged by the club's trainer.

The next day, Cobb was swinging away again—this time during the game for a double and a triple.

Most golf balls thrown onto the field during a game

1,000 golf balls (est.)
Fenway Park, Boston 1949

Hundreds of golf caddies were way out of bounds when they attended a 1949 game as guests of the Boston Red Sox—they pelted the field and the players with 1,000 golf balls!

"The outfield looked like a snowstorm had hit," recalled former Red Sox public-relations director George Sullivan, who at the time was the batboy for the visiting Philadelphia Athletics.

The Red Sox had invited caddies to the game from country clubs all over the area, and they filled up the seats in right field for Caddy Day.

"About halfway through the game, one or two balls were thrown onto the field—then every one of those kids was throwing balls at the A's," said Sullivan.

"The players had to run for cover in the dugout. It lasted about 10 minutes, until the kids finally ran out of golf balls. The maintenance crew kept running out and scooping them up and ducking at the same time.

"The Philadelphia players kept trying to get me to take their caps, go onto the field, and fill them with golf balls so they could use them to play golf later. But I wouldn't do it. I was afraid of getting beaned."

Longest standing ovation for a fan who mooned a team

20 seconds
The Phillie Mooner
Veterans Stadium, Philadelphia   1988

The pathetic last-place Philadelphia Phillies of 1988 were used to seeing themselves behind in games—and on a cool night in May, a disgusted fan let them see *his* behind.

In the eighth inning of a 4–0 loss to the visiting Los Angeles Dodgers, the fan climbed onto a cement wall behind home plate, turned his back to the field, dropped his pants, and mooned the Phils.

As cops led the guy away, the crowd stood and applauded him for 20 seconds. It was the loudest ovation at Veterans Stadium in weeks.

In describing the butt of Phillies fans' outrage, the *Philadelphia Inquirer* said, "Maybe it was an indication that mere words can no longer describe what the 1988 Phillies have become."

Yuckiest Opening Day "pitch"

The Tomato Tosser
Ebbets Field, Brooklyn   1937

The most memorable Opening Day pitch at Ebbets Field came not from a dignitary but a fan. And it wasn't a ball that was thrown, but a ripe tomato.

The target was New York Giants leadoff man Dick Bartell. Dodgers fans had a longstanding hatred of Bartell. In 1933 he spiked Brooklyn first baseman Joe Judge and the next year he spiked shortstop Lonny Frey. In 1936 Bartell got into a wild fistfight with Dodgers pitcher Van Lingle Mungo.

So when the 1937 season rolled around, one unknown fan plotted revenge. As Bartell stepped to the plate to start the game, the Ebbets Field fans booed loudly. Then Mungo, who was the Dodgers' Opening Day pitcher, threw a fastball for a strike.

Bartell stepped out of the batter's box. Suddenly a big soft tomato came whizzing down from the stands. It caught Bartell square in the chest and burst open. "That's *our* Opening Day pitch!" shouted one steamed fan. The stunned batter acted like he'd been shot—and he looked it, too, as the remains of the blood-red tomato ran down his uniform.

The umpire called time so Bartell could run to the clubhouse and change shirts because of his tomato pasting.

Longest game delay caused by fans throwing beer mugs

6 minutes
Wrigley Field, Chicago   1988

Cincinnati Reds center fielder Tracy Jones got "mugged" at Wrigley Field—by Cubs fans who pelted him with so many beer mugs that umpires had to stop the game.

The bleacher bums were getting tanked up after receiving giveaway beer tankards as part of a ballpark promotion to honor Cubs announcer Harry Caray.

Sidelined for three months by a stroke, Caray returned to the microphone on May 19th. Illinois Governor James Thompson proclaimed it "Harry Caray Day"—then unwisely suggested that the Wrigley Field crowd of 28,890 "drink all the Budweiser Harry can't drink."

Fans wasted no time quaffing down a river of ale, using the free tankards. Apparently not realizing the difference between giveaways and throwaways, the bleacher bums tossed their mugs at the Reds' Tracy Jones out in center field. Umpires had to halt the game for six minutes until order was restored.

Jones was not hurt from the mugging. But ever since, whenever he hears the phrase, "This Bud's for you," he ducks.

Most games attended by a pet duck

6 games
Jarry Park, Montreal   1970

The way the last-place Expos played in 1970 was for the birds. Maybe that's why one of the team's noisiest rooters was a duck!

The feathered fan attended his first game when two humans brought the little guy—their pet—to Jarry Park and asked if they could take him inside with them.

"The team policy said no dogs or cats were allowed, but it didn't say anything about ducks," recalled promotions director Roger Savard. "So I told them to buy him a ticket.

"It was really funny because every time the duck

quacked, you could hear him all over the ballpark, and the fans started to quack back."

After six games the duck stopped coming. Maybe he just got tired of seeing the Expos put so many goose eggs up on the scoreboard.

Largest check ever given to a player by a fan

$10,000
"Santa Claus," Lakeland, Florida   1963

Tigers hurler Hank Aguirre thought Christmas had come early when an elderly fan came up to him during spring training in Lakeland, Florida, and thrust a $10,000 check in his hand.

"He was a nicely dressed old man," Aguirre later told reporters. "He said I could cash the check when I got my tenth hit of the year. The check looked legal and everything. But it was signed 'Santa Claus.' "

Aguirre's chances of collecting the cash were slim because in his previous eight years in the major leagues, he had a *total* of only eight hits. Nevertheless, the notoriously weak-hitting Tigers pitcher hung onto the check for five months until he surprised everyone by smacking his tenth hit of the year in August.

After the game, he phoned the bank in Lakeland from which the mystery check had been drawn. Bank officials sadly told Aguirre what he had long suspected: No, Hank, there is no Santa Claus—at least not one with an account there.

Loudest fan ever to annoy a U.S. president

Patsy O'Toole
Griffith Stadium, Washington   1933

President Franklin D. Roosevelt survived polio, World War II, and an assassination attempt. But foghorn fan Patsy O'Toole nearly did him in.

O'Toole drove fellow spectators crazy by screaming the same chants over and over—very loudly. His rallying cry was, "Boy, oh boy, oh boy, oh boy! Keep cool wit' O'Toole!" Then he'd hurl an insult at a player and repeat it constantly.

Although he was a Detroit Tigers fan, O'Toole attended the 1933 World Series between the New York Giants and the Washington Senators. FDR had the misfortune to be seated only a few rows in front of Patsy. Each time the Irishman let out a blast, the president cringed.

After a few minutes of hearing O'Toole's irritating verbal barrage, Roosevelt turned and spoke to a Secret Service agent. The agent then strode to Patsy's seat.

"I'm sure you'd like to do the president a favor," the steely-eyed agent hissed. "He'd like you to move to the other side of the field—and the arrangements have already been made."

The startled O'Toole moved without a peep.

Most fans who played musical instruments during a game

30,000 (est.)
Ebbets Field, Brooklyn   1951

The Brooklyn Dodgers offered free admittance to anyone who brought a musical instrument to a July 1951 game. It proved a great night for music lovers— to stay home!

The big-band sound was never more horrible than the Dodgers' "Musical Unappreciation Night," when about 30,000 fans blasted out "songs" which set music back fifty years.

The fans brought every imaginable instrument including kazoos, harmonicas, and drums. Incredibly, two people even showed up with pianos!

"What a night for music!" exulted Dodgers publicist Irving Rudd. "The weird noises unleashed by the capacity crowd of roof-raisers must have traumatized music lovers for miles around."

Most opponents' home-run balls thrown back onto the field in a season

52 balls
Wrigley Field, Chicago   1990

No fans have more disdain for home runs hit by an opposing player than those who root for the Chicago Cubs.

Even though catching a baseball during a major league game is a prize sought by most every spectator, the Wrigley Field bleacher bums refuse to keep the home run balls of other teams. The fans scornfully toss such balls back onto the field to show their contempt.

Although the tradition dates back to 1969, not until the mid-1980s was it considered mandatory for the bleacherites to throw back home run balls. Failure to do so triggered a chorus of boos and other forms of harassment, such as an unwanted beer bath.

In 1990, the bleacher bums set a new record by tossing back 52 home run balls. (Opponents belted 71.) Even homers hit out of the ballpark were thrown back over the bleachers and onto the field by people walking on the streets.

Since 1984, Jerry Pritikin, known as the Bleacher Preacher, has rewarded fellow bleacher fans who toss back homers. He gives them a certificate and a "fandana," a bandana bearing the Cubs' logo. "It's been fun," said the Cubs' superfan. "I just wish I didn't have to give out so many."

The quietest baseball game ever played

New York Highlanders vs. Jersey City Skeeters
1909

You could have heard a pin drop during a game between the New York Highlanders (forerunners of the Yankees) and the Jersey City Skeeters on April 18, 1909. The crowd not only didn't cheer, they barely said a word. And the players were just as silent.

That's because April 18th was a Sunday. At the time, there were "blue laws" forbidding many activities on the holy day. Several teams had experienced run-ins with the law for playing on Sunday.

Worried about arrest, the Jersey management passed out cards to arriving spectators asking them to keep quiet—and, for God's sake, not to cheer.

To everyone's astonishment, the fans did as they were asked and barely uttered a peep throughout the eerily silent game.

(Psst! The Highlanders won, 6–3).

Most baseball fans to boo Canada's national anthem

52,000 fans (est.)
Yankee Stadium, New York   1985

The New York Yankees brought in vocalist Mary O'Dowd to sing the national anthems of Canada and the United States prior to a game between New York and the Toronto Blue Jays. But Mary left the stadium singing the blues after heartless Yankees fans booed her mercilessly.

It was the start of a crucial four-game series between the first-place Jays and the second-place Yanks, and the New York fans were demanding a sweep by the pinstripers.

As Mary began to warble our northern neighbor's song, Yankee Stadium erupted in loud boos. The booing was a cruel vocal anti-Toronto gesture by disrespectful Yankees fans and was not directed at Mary's singing talent. But Mary was deeply upset. She took the booing personally, stopped in midsong, and ran off the field crying. Mary never returned.

Stadium announcer Bob Sheppard then had to remind the unfeeling fans that Canada and the United States are the best of friends and, besides, it was a group of Canadians who helped U.S. hostages escape from Iran only a few years earlier.

When the Yankees and Blue Jays met three weeks later in Toronto, guess whose national anthem drew some boos from local fans?

Most fans who took a team's promotional giveaway and then didn't stay for the game

500 fans (est.)
Ebbets Field, Brooklyn   1946

One day in 1946, the Brooklyn Dodgers' brass decided they had just the ticket to boost attendance on Ladies' Day. The team announced that 500 pairs of nylon hose would be given away to female fans who attended the next game.

Since nylon stockings were difficult to buy in those post-World War II days, team officials figured lots of ladies would jump at the chance to get a pair of hose.

Did they ever! A screaming mob of 2,434 gals came storming into Ebbets Field—most of whom wouldn't have known a baseball from a basketball.

But to the Dodgers' dismay, most of the 500 women who were given the stockings promptly turned on their pretty heels and went home. So did many of the other 1,934 gals who missed out on the hose and left empty-legged.

Only "preacher" expelled from a ballpark for throwing a Frisbee

Jerry Pritikin
Wrigley Field, Chicago   1987

Diehard Chicago Cubs fan Jerry Pritikin, the "Bleacher Preacher" of Wrigley Field, caught holy hell from a security guard when he flung a Frisbee to New York Mets pitcher Roger McDowell.

Pritikin and McDowell occasionally played Frisbee before Cubs-Mets games. Each time the hurler came to Chicago, he always looked for Jerry in the stands and said, "Where's your Frisbee?"

But when the Preacher cocked his arm to throw out the first disc on September 22, 1987, a stadium cop yelled "Stop!"

"I flung it anyway," said Jerry, a Cubs fan for 42 years. The Frisbee Patrol hustled the Preacher out of the stadium faster than you can say, "Amen." He spent the game glumly sitting on a bench outside the ballpark.

"They could have just confiscated the Frisbee," he said bitterly. "After all the years I've been out there and cheering, this is the reward I get."

Until that day, he'd aways worn a shirt that read: JERRY PRITIKIN, BLEACHER PREACHER, THE GOSPEL OF THE CUBS.

At the next game, his shirt read: THIS SPACE FOR RENT.

Smallest crowd to see an All-Star Game

25,556 fans
Braves Field, Boston   1936

The press hyped the 1936 All-Star Game so much that fans stayed away in droves!

With the midseason classic at Braves Field in Boston featuring a host of legends including Joe DiMaggio, Lou Gehrig, Carl Hubbell, and Dizzy Dean, local newspapers and radio stations went wild with frenzied—and untrue—reports that tickets were in short supply.

One newspaper said tickets were "worth their weight in gold," discouraging thousands of fans from going to the ballpark. On game day a radio broadcaster reported that the huge number of fans en route to the park had caused a gigantic traffic jam. That kept even more would-be spectators away.

It wasn't until after the game that furious fans learned there hadn't been a traffic jam at all and, in fact, more than 10,000 tickets had gone unsold!

Most fans' All-Star votes for a retired player

729,249 votes
Mike Schmidt, Philadelphia Phillies   1989

Mike Schmidt was the runaway winner in the fans' voting for the starting third baseman on the National League's 1989 All-Star team. But there was one hitch —Schmidt had already retired earlier in the season.

Even though he was out of baseball, fans still made him the leading vote-getter at third base. National League manager Tommy Lasorda had no choice but to ignore the fans' wishes. He selected Howard Johnson of the New York Mets to start in Schmidt's spot.

Despite his retirement, Schmidt showed up at the game wearing his Philadelphia Phillies uniform. He received the loudest and longest ovation from the fans when he stepped onto the field during the player introductions.

"This is a bonus," he said. "I'll always remember this. I never thought this would happen."

Greatest number of ticket holders who *didn't* see a World Series game

6,000 fans (est.)
Municipal Stadium, Cleveland 1948

A stupendous 86,288 rabid fans poured into Cleveland Municipal Stadium to watch Game 5 of the 1948 World Series. But about 6,000 of those paying customers didn't even catch a glimpse of the players.

After the stadium's 78,000 seats were filled, more than 8,000 fans were clamoring to get in. So they each paid $5 and were hustled to a standing-room-only area behind the outfield fence, where they spent the entire game.

Since it was impossible to see through the crowd packed close to the fence, some 6,000 fans watched nothing but the hair growing on the heads of people in front of them.

And, incredibly, almost nobody complained!

One Cleveland fan, who brought along a portable

radio, explained: "I just wanted to be a part of the scene and hear the roar of the crowd."

The unseeing spectators griped a bit more when their beloved Indians were scalped by the Boston Braves that day, 11–5. But the fans' blind devotion paid off. Cleveland bounced back to win the World Series.

Smallest turnout for a game involving a big-league team

6 fans
Philadelphia Athletics vs. University of Delaware
1944

A raging blizzard suddenly swept into the Athletics' spring training camp in Wilmington, Delaware, just before a game with the University of Delaware's baseball team in 1944. Despite heavy snow and bitter cold, the game was played anyway—but only a half-dozen shivering spectators showed up to watch.

The Athletics won, 2–0, in what definitely was not a heated contest.

After the most piddling turnout in major league history, the frozen A's abandoned Wilmington the following year for warmer spring training climes in Florida.

Most fans who showed up for a rained-out game at the Astrodome

20 fans
Houston   1976

The officials of Houston's Astrodome assured fans that no game at the indoor park would ever be canceled by rain. But on June 16, 1976, the impossible happened—and 20 diehard fans received rain checks to prove it.

That day a huge cloudburst dumped seven inches of rain on the city, flooding the area surrounding the Astrodome. The players were already inside, but the umpires—and just about everyone else—couldn't reach the stadium.

However, the deluge didn't stop 20 clever fans from canoeing to the gate. Once inside, they were rewarded for their perseverance. The fans were treated by the club to a free meal and given rain checks that team officials thought would never be needed at the 'Dome.

Most Groucho Marx look-alikes to watch a major league game

36,716 look-alikes
Kingdome, Seattle   1982

It was a spectacle to behold when the entire crowd in Seattle's Kingdome sported eyeglasses with bushy brows and big noses during a 1982 game.

To try to boost attendance, the Mariners held a "Funny Nose and Glasses Night" and gave away a set of Groucho Marx–type spectacles—complete with a crooked nose and black mustache—to every fan.

The stunt worked. A whopping 36,716 spectators—Seattle's biggest crowd of the season—turned out to claim their free gift.

But if the Mariners expected four-eyed fans to help them win, the club was looking at the world through rose-colored glasses. The Yankees easily knocked off the M's, 9–4.

After the game, Mariners marketing director Jeff Odenfeld had a slight problem. He had a few freebies left over. So Odenfeld went on television and said, "If anyone would like to buy 10,000 funny noses and glasses, please get in touch with me."

Adding
Insult to Injury
WARPED RECORDS OF INJURIES

Most games missed due to cooking his own foot

16 games
Joe DiMaggio, New York Yankees   1936

Slugging sensation Joe DiMaggio was really the toast of the town in his rookie season—he baked his left foot.

The freak injury happened in the Yankees' spring training camp in 1936 when DiMaggio, who had been batting a stupendous .600 in the exhibition season, lay down on a training table with a heating device on his left foot.

He was hoping to relieve pain in his foot, which was

swollen from being stepped on by an infielder during a game. Joe dozed off on the training table . . . and when he woke up, his foot looked like a well-done side of beef.

Doctors had to lance and drain two huge blisters. Then they sent DiMaggio to bed for two days. His first-degree burns healed so slowly that he missed the first 16 games of the regular season.

Joe was depressed. But when docs finally gave him the OK to play, the future "Mr. Coffee" perked right up and hotfooted it back into the lineup.

First game ever called because of potential flatulence

Niagara vs. Buffalo   1859

The Niagara Baseball Club was declared a 24–22 winner over the Buffalo Baseball Club in an 1859 contest that didn't go all the way. The official scorebook included this odd entry: "Game called after five innings—[Niagara shortstop] Tom Shiels filled with gas and unable to play longer."

Earliest injury to a player on Opening Day

3 minutes before the game
George Myatt, Washington Senators   1946

Third baseman George Myatt was looking forward to a spring filled with baseball when a fall filled him with pain and disappointment instead.

Thanks to too much enthusiasm, Myatt was knocked out of the lineup by a bad spill before he even made it on the field for the opening game of the 1946 season.

After President Harry S Truman threw out the first ball at Griffith Stadium, the Senators raced up the dugout steps to the roar of the crowd. But Myatt was so excited he didn't watch where he was going—and tripped over his own feet.

As teammates watched in shock, he sprawled backward down the steps, fracturing a bone in his ankle.

The woebegone third sacker was put out of action and replaced by Sherry Robertson—the first substitute of a season that was yet to open.

Most postseason games missed by a player injured by a runaway tarpaulin

10 games
Vince Coleman, St. Louis Cardinals   1985

Base-stealing superstar Vince Coleman was knocked out of the 1985 National League Championship Series and the World Series because he was struck by a runaway tarpaulin.

The fleet-footed Cardinals outfielder was doing stretching exercises on the field at St. Louis's Busch Stadium just before the fourth playoff game against the Los Angeles Dodgers when rain began to fall.

A member of the grounds crew quickly pulled a lever activating a 120-foot-wide cylinder that rolled a canvas tarpaulin over the infield. The cylinder went rumbling across the field—and slammed right into Coleman and kept on going for several yards.

Coleman, who was facing the opposite direction and didn't see it coming, was knocked to the ground. His foot was bruised and a bone in his left knee was chipped. He missed the rest of the playoffs, which the Cardinals won, and all of the World Series, which St. Louis lost.

The runaway tarp gave new meaning to the term hit and run.

Most stitches needed by a superstar's mom after being struck by a foul ball

6 stitches
Bob Feller's mother 1939

The parents of Cleveland hurler Bob Feller journeyed from their home in Van Meter, Iowa, to Chicago to watch their son pitch against the White Sox.

It was Mother's Day, 1939. It was also both a memorable and painful day for Mrs. Lena Feller.

She was sitting in a box seat along the first-base line when White Sox batter Marv Owen fouled off a pitch in the third inning. It sailed into the stands and struck Mrs. Feller smack in the head. The impact broke the poor lady's glasses and opened a cut above her right eye that required six stitches to close.

Feller rushed into the stands to check on his mom. When he saw that she was not seriously injured, he returned to the mound and got revenge on the batter who had done the dirty deed. The hurler struck out Owen and went on to beat the White Sox, 9–4.

When it came to somebody hurting his mother, Bob was not a jolly good Feller.

Only pitcher to break a knuckle by hitting a toilet seat

Jim Barr, California Angels   1979

Here's the poop on why hurler Jim Barr sat out the 1979 playoffs: He punched a toilet seat and flushed his chances of playing by breaking his pitching hand!

The silly stunt took place on the night the Angels clinched their division by beating the second-place Kansas City Royals in Anaheim.

"We'd been battling Kansas City for the title, and Royals owner Ewing Kauffman had come out on the radio saying we didn't deserve to win and a bunch of other stuff," recalled Barr, a 10-game winner for the Angels that year.

"When we won the division, we had a big celebration at a bar near the stadium where we hung out.

"An Angels fan brought a toilet seat into the bar with a sign attached that said FLUSH THE ROYALS. When the lid was lifted, there was a picture of Kauffman inside.

"I wasn't feeling any pain by then, so I punched the seat, thinking it was cardboard. But it was a real toilet seat—and I fractured the little knuckle on my pitching hand. I was out the rest of the season. That little stunt really finished me off."

Most fans injured due to a pitcher's poor performance

3 fans
Kirby Higbe, Pittsburgh Pirates   1948

Pitcher Kirby Higbe took a beating when he faced the Philadelphia Phillies on June 13, 1948. But his fans had an even worse day. Thanks to Higbe's horrible hurling, three spectators got hurt just watching the game.

In the first inning, the visiting Phillies pounced on Higbe like lions on a slab of raw meat, getting five hits and three runs. In the upper tier of the stands at Forbes Field, a fanatic Higbe fan named Thomas Muenzer got more upset with each hit until finally he jumped to his feet screaming for Higbe to do better.

As Muenzer was jumping up and down, he lost his balance and fell over the railing—and landed on two people below. Luckily, the trio was not seriously injured (after all, they were "diehard" fans). They were taken to the hospital, treated, and released.

Muenzer then hurried back to the ballpark because, he said, "I want to see more of Higbe's pitching." But Kirby had been yanked from the game—by the very same hit that had sent Meunzer tumbling over the rail.

Most times a pitcher was knocked out in one game

2 times
Freddie Fitzsimmons, New York Giants 1931

Balls zeroed in on luckless Freddie Fitzsimmons like meat-seeking missiles during a 1931 game against the Brooklyn Dodgers.

He was pitching to Babe Herman when the Dodgers batter sent a screaming liner straight back at him. Instead of ducking, fearless Fred tried to catch the ball —and got nailed in the belly so hard he was actually lifted into the air.

Freddie collapsed like a punctured balloon and lay unconscious for several minutes. When he finally woke up, he wobbled unsteadily to his feet and then demanded to return to the mound.

The hurler was still groggy when he came to bat in the next inning. The first pitch sailed high and inside. Too woozy to get out of the way, Freddie caught the ball square on the skull, giving the Dodgers their second knockout of the game.

A few minutes later, Fitzsimmons rose to his feet and announced, "They haven't made a ball yet that could make me say quits." Freddie stayed in the game, but he had no recollection of what happened.

Most days unable to pitch after a trip to the bathroom

10 days
Dave Goltz, California Angels   1982

In one of the weirdest freak accidents in baseball history, Angels pitcher Dave Goltz was sidelined for a week and a half after slicing open a finger—while going to the bathroom.

In 1982, the ace right-hander felt the call of nature the night before he was due to pitch against the Boston Red Sox. As he sat on the commode, Goltz reached for some toilet paper and discovered the roll was bare.

He stuck his right hand up inside the two-roll dispenser to grab some paper from the spare roll.

"He cut a three-inch gash in his right index finger on a little screw or piece of metal," recalled Angels trainer Rick Smith.

The bathroom injury healed so slowly that Dave couldn't take the mound for 10 days.

Most starts missed from flicking sunflower seeds

2 starts
Greg Harris, Texas Rangers   1987

Rangers right-hander Greg Harris was scratched from two starts after he was stricken by the most dreaded disease known to hurlers—"sunflower-seed elbow."

During a game between starts, Harris began playfully flicking sunflower seeds from the dugout to a friend in the box seats. Soon afterward, Harris's right elbow began to swell and hurt so badly that he couldn't throw.

Harris had no choice but to rest his seedy arm through two scheduled starts. "I know," he said sheepishly. "It sounds ridiculous."

Longest hospital stay by a pitcher after being hit by a warm-up throw from the catcher

10 days
Ken Sanders, New York Mets   1975

Mets reliever Ken Sanders went straight from the mound to the medics after he was beaned by his own catcher.

Disaster struck as the pitcher took his first warm-up toss in a 1975 game against the Los Angeles Dodgers. Catcher John Stearns caught the ball and then fired it back to the mound, where it slammed into Sanders's face.

"The Mets had a glass partition in the screen behind home plate so the cameras could film through it," the hurler recalled. "Evidently I lost the ball in the glare of that partition. I never saw it coming.

"The ball broke my nose and a bone in my cheek. I was in the hospital for 10 days."

Sanders, who fully recovered, said he didn't blame his catcher. However, he added, "Stearns really fired it back at me. He was a former college quarterback, real gung-ho. Everything he did was physical and aggressive, which is fine. But I thought at the time, 'Gee, why'd he do that? I'm on his side.' "

Most times struck by foul tips in one inning before being carried off the field

3 times
Larry Napp, American League   1960

In one pain-filled inning, plate umpire Larry Napp was knocked out of action after being struck by three hard-hit foul tips.

It happened in the ninth inning of a 1960 game between the visiting New York Yankees and the Baltimore Orioles. Yankees slugger Roger Maris first felled Napp, a former prizefighter, with a foul that slammed right into his groin. Napp doubled over in pain, but then he shook it off and resumed his position behind the plate.

Mickey Mantle, the next batter up, then stunned Napp with a foul tip that nearly caved in his mask. The umpire staggered, but refused to go down.

However, Mantle's next foul smashed into Napp's groin a second time. That was too much. The ump collapsed unconscious right across home plate.

Napp was carried off to the Orioles' clubhouse where the team doctor revived him. The tough ump awoke, claiming he was ready to go back to work. Added Napp, "I don't think I was ever that hurt in the boxing ring."

The Worse for Wear
WARPED RECORDS OF UNIFORMS
AND EQUIPMENT

Most innings played in an overcoat

8½ innings
Joe Werrick, Louisville Colonels   1887

Third baseman Joe Werrick once wore a long overcoat nearly all the way through a major league game.

He didn't do it as a joke. Joe had the flu and his
doctor had ordered him not to play on that chilly day
in 1887. But Joe's Louisville team desperately needed
him, so he threw a big overcoat over his uniform and
took the field.

The crowd had a field day laughing at the coat-clad
figure at third. Luckily, few balls came Joe's way, so
his coat didn't hamper his fielding.

But it was a different story when he tried to bat. Standing there in his coat with his red nose dripping like a leaky faucet, Joe couldn't hit anything. He struck out his first three visits to the plate.

When Louisville came up to bat in the last of the ninth, the score was tied. There were two outs and two men on base when Joe got up. He wiped his runny nose on his coat sleeve, swung at the first ball, and missed miserably.

Louisville fans begged him to take off the overcoat. Joe realized that was his only chance. He shed the coat—and on the very next pitch, the Sultan of Snot hit a game-winning triple!

Only player to wear the name of his hometown on the back of his uniform

Bill Voiselle, Boston Braves–Chicago Cubs
1947–1950

When pitcher Big Bill Voiselle was traded by the New York Giants to the Boston Braves in 1947, the hurler decided it was a good time to ballyhoo his hometown.

So even though players back then usually wore numbers between 1 and 50, Voiselle asked for a special number on the back of his uniform—No. 96. That's because the hurler hailed from the tiny town of Ninety-Six, South Carolina, and he wanted everyone to know it.

At the time, Voiselle's number was the highest in baseball. But in 1977, Oakland Athletics outfielder Willie Crawford topped it. Knowing it would be his last year in the bigs, Willie wanted to be remembered for something, so he wore the highest number ever in the major leagues—No. 99.

Most games played with yellow balls

4 games
Brooklyn Dodgers   1938, 1939

Baseball's rule book specifies that only a "white horsehide" ball can be used in the major leagues. But the Dodgers played four games in the 1930s using baseballs that looked like they'd contracted a bad case of jaundice.

Brooklyn's general manager, Larry MacPhail, came up with the idea of trying a different color ball. He suggested dandelion yellow. On August 2, 1938, the Dodgers and St. Louis Cardinals became the first teams to give the new colored ball a shot. Brooklyn won, 6–2, at Ebbets Field.

In 1939 the yellow ball was used in three more Dodgers games, two against the Cardinals (which St. Louis won, 12–0 and 5–2), and one against the Chicago Cubs (which Brooklyn won, 10–4).

After those games, the sickly looking yellow ball was never used again in a major league game, although Charles O. Finley had his Oakland Athletics play with orange baseballs in some spring training games in 1973.

Most expensive T-shirt worn by a pitcher

$250
Johnny Allen, Cleveland Indians   1938

Before a 1938 game against the Boston Red Sox, Cleveland hurler Johnny Allen sliced the sleeve of his sweatshirt so that his pitches would look like they were emerging from a tangled whirl of tattered strips.

But umpire Bill McGowan said the flapping, frayed sleeve was distracting batters. The ump gave Allen an ultimatum: Cut off the tattered sleeve, change shirts, or get thrown out of the game.

Without a word, Allen left the field. When he failed to return after five minutes, manager Ossie Vitt found him in the showers. The stubborn and angry pitcher defied Vitt's order to return to the mound and was fined $250.

The punishment didn't hurt Allen one bit. In fact, he actually made money on the fine. He sold the shirt for $500 to a Cleveland clothing store which displayed it in its show window.

Allen eventually gave the shirt off his back to the Baseball Hall of Fame. The ragged article of clothing is still on display in Cooperstown.

Most times a player wore a number that was retired

2 times
Cliff Mapes, New York Yankees   1948–1951

Both numbers worn by outfielder Cliff Mapes during his 3½ year stint with the New York Yankees were retired. But Mapes didn't get too excited about it—because the shirts were hung up in honor of other players!

Mapes was assigned No. 3 when he joined the Yankees in 1948. But that was Babe Ruth's old number, and when Ruth died that year his number was retired by the club.

So Mapes was assigned No. 7, which he wore until he was traded to the St. Louis Browns in 1951. Then along came Mickey Mantle, who wore the number—and eventually number 7 was retired in Mantle's honor.

The only retirement Mapes ever saw was his own after a postbaseball career with a fertilizer company.

Most innings played in a raincoat

2 innings
Germany Schaefer, Detroit Tigers   1906

Trailing the Cleveland Indians, 5–0, the visiting Detroit Tigers were hoping a steady drizzle would turn into a downpour and cancel the game before it had gone the required 4½ innings.

In the bottom of the fourth, the rain became heavier, but umpire Bill Evans wouldn't call the game. So in the top of the fifth, Detroit's Germany Schaefer strolled out to his second-base position wearing a long rubber raincoat that covered him from head to foot.

As the crowd roared with laughter, Schaefer kept the raincoat on all through the fifth and six innings, when the game finally was called because of the rain. Cleveland was awarded the victory.

In another game in which Detroit was losing, a drizzle began in the fifth inning, so Germany tried to convince the umpire to cancel the game. The fun-loving Tiger stepped to the plate clad in a rain slicker—plus hip boots and an umbrella!

Umpire Silk O'Loughlin ordered Schaefer to take off his crazy costume. Germany argued with the ump and then gave up. So Schaefer folded the umbrella and carried it back to the bench. Then, returning to the plate, he sat down and slowly began taking off his hip boots.

By the time he was finished, the drizzle had given way to a downpour and the umps called the game—which was exactly what Germany had wanted.

Biggest bat ever used in a major league game

5 feet 10 inches long
Bill Lange, Chicago Cubs   1894

After striking out twice in a game against the New York Giants, Cubs outfielder Bill Lange tried to change his luck by switching to a bat nearly six feet long!

The crowd at New York's Polo Grounds roared with laughter when Lange came to the plate with the monster bat, which had been presented to the Cubs by

Frank McKee, manager of the Madison Square Theater, as a joke.

In the eighth inning, Lange begged umpire John McQuaid to let him use the giant stick. The Giants, who were enjoying a comfortable six-run lead, didn't object, so the umpire gave him the go-ahead.

With a huge *oof*! Lange swung and connected, knocking a slow grounder to first baseman Jack Doyle. But Doyle fumbled the ball for an error.

The next batter, Charlie Irwin, spoke softly and asked if he could carry the big stick to the plate. But Giants manager Monte Ward objected—and the titanic timber, a full 2 feet 4 inches longer than a regulation bat, was retired with full honors.

Dandiest player in major league history

Art "The Great" Shires, Chicago White Sox–
Washington Senators–Boston Braves   1928–1932

First baseman Art Shires was the fanciest dresser baseball ever saw. He owned so many dandy duds, he could have outfitted a small army of men-about-town —with a few hats left over.

When Shires joined the White Sox in 1928, he brought along a wardrobe that included 50 suits, 100 hats, 40 pairs of spats, 300 neckties, and 20 canes— plus a morning suit, six tuxedos, and sports attire for yachting, golf, riding, and motoring!

Oh yeah, he also brought along two baseball uniforms . . . both filthy.

Only superstar ever to own a bat made out of a railroad tie

Babe Ruth, New York Yankees   1929

Babe Ruth owned one of the most unusual bats in baseball history—crafted out of an old railroad tie dug up in a steamy Central American jungle.

The tie—sawed out of tough *lignum vitae* wood—had been used on the railroad line built across the Isthmus of Panama in 1850 at the height of California's gold rush.

It had lain buried in the jungle for 79 years when civilian workers for the U.S. Army unearthed it in 1929. They didn't know what to do with it until someone got the bright idea to have the tie made into a bat for Ruth. The Bambino was presented with the odd bat in a special ceremony at the start of the 1929 season.

If Babe had wielded the lumber, he would have given new meaning to the term "he tied one on." But the bat was a little too heavy to use in a game.

Zaniest uniform ever worn by a captain delivering the lineup card to home plate

Doug Rader, Houston Astros   1974

When the San Diego Padres held a "Short-Order Cooks Night" at their stadium, Astros captain Doug Rader cooked up a special gag for the occasion. He waltzed out to home plate wearing a tall chef's hat and a cooking apron!

The fun-loving redhead was carrying a frying skillet

with the Astros' lineup card inside. He casually flipped the card like a pancake as he walked to home plate for the pregame meeting with the umpires.

The crowd, which included more than 1,300 short-order cooks, burst into laughter and applause. That was a relief to Doug—because he was expecting the cooks to boil him in oil.

Earlier in the year, Rader touched off a tirade of protests from the chefs over an offhand remark. When Padres owner Ray Kroc called the San Diego team's playing "stupid," Rader responded, "He must think he's dealing with a bunch of short-order cooks." San Diego's frymen raised an angry uproar, taking his remark as an insult to their profession. Doug apologized, but the chefs weren't appeased.

But when he dressed as one of their own, the cooks forgave Doug and turned down the heat.

Only player to wear his entire birthdate on his uniform

Carlos May, Chicago White Sox   1968–1975

White Sox outfielder Carlos May was the first and only player to wear his entire birthdate on his uniform.

The back of his jersey displayed his last name— May—over his number—17. Carlos was born in 1948 in Birmingham, Alabama, on May 17th.

Most innings played in formal attire

9 innings
Wes Fisler, Philadelphia Phillies   1876

Baseball uniforms seemed so ... well ... *tacky* to Wes Fisler. To show fans he was really a classy guy, he played nine innings dressed to the nines.

The Phillies' first baseman went an entire game in 1876 decked out in a Prince Albert coat, striped gray trousers, black patent-leather shoes, and a fancy white formal shirt.

Of course, his dandy demeanor was offset a bit by the fact that Wes topped off the fancy attire with a regulation baseball cap!

Wackiest uniform number request

No. 337
Bill "Spaceman" Lee, Boston Red Sox   1973

Pitcher Bill Lee, who had been wearing No. 37 on his Red Sox uniform, asked for No. 337 at the start of the 1973 season.

Although he was turned down, inquiring minds wanted to know why he wanted this particular number. The Spaceman explained, "Because if you turn 337 upside down, it spells 'LEE.' And then I could stand on my head and people would know me right away."

No's for News

WARPED RECORDS OF THE MEDIA

Most fibs told by a radio announcer during one at-bat

17 fibs
Ronald Reagan, Des Moines, Iowa   1936

Ronald Reagan started out as a baseball broadcaster at radio station WHO in Des Moines, Iowa. But even way back then it was obvious he had the makings of a politician.

The future president was re-creating a Chicago Cubs game from an ongoing wire service account of each pitch. Reagan made his own sound effects—such as the sound of a bat hitting a ball—to give listeners the impression that he was actually at the game.

Suddenly, just as Cubs star Stan Hack got up to bat, the transmission line from Wrigley Field broke down.

But quick-thinking Reagan kept the play-by-play going. He told rapt listeners that Hack had fouled off the pitch ... then fouled off another ... then another. . . .

By the time the line was fixed and Reagan got back to the real action, he had listeners believing Hack had fouled off 17 straight pitches!

Most number of violent attacks on players in a baseball film

5 assaults
Death on the Diamond   *1934*

Baseball players had a lot more to worry about than pop flies in the 1934 film *Death on the Diamond*. They were dropping like flies!

In the murder mystery, a star pitcher for the St. Louis Cardinals was shot as he raced home with the winning run, another Cards pitcher was strangled in the clubhouse, and the catcher went to an early grave after eating a poison-laced hot dog.

Hit men, hired by gamblers, also shot up a taxi carrying a third hurler. Later they tried to murder him with a bomb. But the pitcher—played by Robert Young, later TV's "Marcus Welby, M.D."—managed to survive.

Oddly enough, nobody tried to kill the ump.

Highest spot over the infield
from which a game was broadcast

208 feet
Lindsey Nelson, Houston   1965

If a ball had hit broadcaster Lindsey Nelson in the head during an April 28, 1965, game he was covering, it still would have been in play—because he was hanging 208 feet in the air directly over the infield.

The plucky play-by-play man for the New York Mets spent the whole game perched in a gondola suspended from the roof of Houston's Astrodome.

Under the stadium's ground rules, a ball that hits any part of the roof is still in play. Oddly enough, Nelson and his gondola were considered part of the roof —so they were included in the rules.

Using binoculars, Nelson did a play-by-play broadcast via walkie-talkie during the seventh and eighth innings of the game between the Mets and Astros. He provided color commentary the rest of the time.

The announcer took a scorecard aloft with him, but didn't take anything to write with. He was afraid that if he dropped a pen it would rocket down and impale a player on the field below.

Nelson probably figured that being on the air while in the air would bring high ratings. But it didn't bring his Mets any luck—they went down to defeat, 12–9.

Most innings in which the play-by-play announcers used the wrong pitcher's name

6 innings
Mel Allen, Phil Rizzuto, New York   1961

Listeners of a New York Yankees broadcast were led to believe that Minnesota Twins hurler Jack Kralick was pitching a great game. That is, until it was discovered he wasn't even on the field—he was sitting on the bench.

Although Kralick originally was listed as the starting pitcher, Twins manager Sam Mele decided at the last minute to start Jim Kaat, another lefthander, in the 1961 contest. But nobody bothered to inform sportscasters Mel Allen and Phil Rizzuto in the Yankees' broadcast booth.

So for six innings the duo unwittingly described the play-by-play exploits of Jack Kralick, a pitcher who was in the dugout the whole time!

It wasn't until the end of the sixth that Rizzuto finally took a closer look at the Twins' hurler on the mound. "Hey," he whispered to Allen as he turned red in the face, "we've had the wrong pitcher all night!"

Hey, Mel, "How 'bout that!"

First baseball player to gripe about being quoted accurately

Pedro Guerrero, St. Louis Cardinals 1989

During an informal bull session with reporters in the clubhouse, Cardinals first baseman Pedro Guerrero claimed that he hadn't been treated fairly by most everyone when he played for the Los Angeles Dodgers.

He said Dodgers manager Tommy Lasorda had treated him "like a dog" before shipping him off to St. Louis in a 1988 trade.

Guerrero then complained that the L.A. sportswriters had caused him problems. His beef: "Sometimes they write what I say and not what I mean."

Longest time on TV with mustard on the face

12 seconds
Bob Costas, Boston 1986

Glib commentator Bob Costas confesses that his most embarrassing moment came as he was giving a brief wrap-up at the end of a Boston Red Sox–Chicago White Sox game at Fenway Park.

"Just as I said, 'Hi, Bob Costas here with Tony Kubek,' a gust of wind blew a hot dog wrapper right onto my face—and it stuck.

"I tried casually to toss the wrapper away, but the next day when I watched the tape, I realized I was talking for 12 seconds with mustard smeared all over my nose!"

Longest distance that a sportswriter was dragged by his feet on the clubhouse floor

60 feet
Kenny Hand, Houston Post   *1980*

Houston Astros beat reporter Kenny Hand was literally swept off his feet when the Astros beat the Dodgers in Los Angeles in a playoff game to capture the division title.

When Hand walked into the victorious clubhouse, the players were celebrating by swigging champagne and engaging in horseplay. Houston outfielder Cesar Cedeno then told Hand that he wanted to teach the reporter how to slide.

"Cedeno threw me down on the floor and grabbed my ankles," Hand recalled. "Tables were overturned and there was champagne, beer, potato salad, mustard, urine, and vomit all over the floor. It looked like *Animal House.*

"Cedeno then dragged me all over the clubhouse floor from one end of the room to the other—about 60 feet. When he finally let go, I was soaking wet and smelled like a garbage can."

To make matters worse, Hand hadn't brought along a change of clothes and he and the team had to fly out that night from Los Angeles to Philadelphia for the start of the championship series with the Phillies.

"The flight attendants almost didn't let me get on the plane because I really stunk," said Hand. "I reached in my pocket for my ticket and pulled out some potato salad. I never dried off and had to ride that way on a five-hour flight. The other writers felt like throwing up when they smelled me.

"Being dragged 60 feet must be some kind of record that will stand forever. Who the hell would be stupid enough to want to break it?"

Longest walk in baseball history

315 miles
Jim Rooker, Pennsylvania 1989

Pittsburgh broadcaster Jim Rooker stuck his feet in his mouth when the Pirates jumped off to a huge 10–0 lead over the Phillies at Philadelphia. He proclaimed to his audience, "If the Bucs blow this one, I'll walk back to Pittsburgh."

The Bucs immediately fell apart and lost, 15–11.

Rooker hoped his vow would be forgotten. But gleeful fans started phoning in and saying, "Hit the road, Jim." So the broadcaster had to go through with it. But to make the journey worthwhile, he first took cash pledges.

He started the trek at the entrance to Philadelphia's Veterans Stadium and walked to home plate in Three Rivers Stadium. "It was 315 miles—which for me was 314 too many!" said Rooker.

"The upside was that we raised $81,000 for charity. So even though I ended up with my share of blisters, it was worth it in the long run." Make that the long walk.

Biggest suit filed by a hurler wrongly blamed on TV for throwing a gopher ball

$3.5 million
Art Ditmar   1985

Former New York Yankees pitcher Art Ditmar wanted the world to know the truth. He was *not* the pitcher who gave up the winning home run in the 1960 World Series, despite what an Anheuser-Busch TV commercial said.

It was the Yankees' Ralph Terry who threw the famed gopher ball that Pittsburgh Pirates hero Bill Mazeroski belted for the Series-winning blast.

The beer commercial, which aired during the 1985 World Series, showed fans listening to a 1960 broadcast in which announcer Chuck Thompson re-created the call which erroneously said Ditmar was pitching to Mazeroski.

"Anheuser-Busch was real apologetic about it and offered to settle for $10,000, but I turned them down," Ditmar recalled. "What upset me was that even after they'd been told the commercial was wrong they kept on using it.

"I know I didn't have a good Series. I had two bad starts. But I shouldn't have been blamed for the game-losing pitch. It just wasn't right to keep using my name when they [the beer company] knew better."

So Ditmar sued for $3.5 million, claiming that his reputation had been damaged.

But the outcome in court was the same as Ditmar's fate in the Series—a bitter loss. "The judge was a woman who didn't know anything about the game," said Ditmar. "She said I wasn't defamed since one home run was just like another."

Longest time a sportscaster interviewed players with his pants rolled up

10 minutes
Jack Moran, Cincinnati   1961

Cincinnati TV sportscaster Jack Moran was doing a live pregame broadcast in front of the Reds' dugout when he became the embarrassed target of a prank by shortstop Eddie Kasko.

"Moran was standing there with a microphone interviewing players, managers, and so on," recalled Pat Harmon, sports editor of the *Cincinnati Post*.

"Then Kasko comes out of the dugout on his hands and knees, goes over behind Moran, and rolls up Moran's pants above his knees. And Moran can't do anything about it because he's on the air!"

TV viewers were puzzled when the broadcast was interrupted by waves of laughter. They were seeing Moran only from the waist up—while fans at the game were watching him get caught with his pants up!

Worst stat uttered by a player-turned-announcer

Duane Kuiper, San Francisco   1988

Going into baseball was the right decision for Duane Kuiper. He would have starved as a math teacher.

During a radio broadcast of a 1988 San Francisco

Giants–Los Angeles Dodgers game, Kuiper enlightened his audience with this nugget:

"[Giants hurler] Dave Dravecky has now thrown 66 pitches through six innings. It doesn't take a very smart guy to figure out that's 12 an inning."

Smallest radio station ever to win a team's broadcast rights

10 watts
KALX-FM University of California at Berkeley   1978

When the Oakland Athletics opened the 1978 season at home, only the fans in the ballpark and those with radios in a three-mile range of the University of California at Berkeley campus were able to catch all the action.

That's because A's owner Charlie Finley sold radio rights for the first 16 A's games to KALX-FM, the school's tiny 10-watt student-operated campus station.

"The season started before we had our contract with our regular A's radio station worked out, so I sold the broadcast rights to the school," Finley explained. "They didn't have much coverage, though."

Larry Baer, a 20-year-old political science major handled the play-by-play. Station officials refused to discuss the financial arrangements, but the crafty Finley revealed that he negotiated a contract that ran to one figure.

"I let them have the rights for a dollar," he recalled. "It was either let the campus station broadcast our games or get up on a soapbox and do it myself."

Longest time before broadcasters recognized the third out

10 minutes
Rusty Staub, Fran Healy, New York   1989

It took 10 minutes before Mets announcers Rusty Staub and Fran Healy realized that the great play they had just witnessed and described to their audience never really happened.

In a 1989 game in San Francisco, the Mets and Giants were tied, 1–1, in the bottom of the ninth with two outs and Giants runner Ernest Riles on first base.

On a 1-and-2 pitch to Kirt Manwaring, Riles took off for second. Manwaring swung and missed, retiring the side. But for some reason, catcher Barry Lyons whipped the ball to second base anyway, trying to nail Riles.

The ball sailed into center field, so Riles raced to third, then rounded the bag and steamed for the plate. Center fielder Lenny Dykstra scooped up the ball and rifled it home where Lyons tagged the runner . . . for the *fourth* out of the inning.

Lyons, who later claimed he knew the inning was over when Manwaring struck out, said he threw to second for practice. Dykstra said he knew the side was retired but instinct made him make the play at the plate.

Meanwhile, up in the broadcast booth, Healy and Staub were excitedly rehashing the dramatic play that "saved" the Mets from a ninth-inning loss.

Not until 10 minutes later—midway through the 10th inning—did Healy and Staub get word that the play was meaningless because Manwaring had already made the third out. Imagine how even more embarrassing it would have been for them had Riles beaten the throw to the plate!

Most outs recorded on a play that didn't count

3 outs
New York Mets   1967

The Mets were leading the Pittsburgh Pirates, 1–0, in the top of the ninth of a 1967 game at Shea Stadium. But the Pirates had the bases loaded with no outs. The crowd was going nuts as the tension mounted. Then clutch hitter Bill Mazeroski stepped to the plate—and banged into a game-ending triple play!

It was the kind of dramatic finish you only see in the movies. In fact, it was in the movies—because the triple play had been staged for a scene in the film, *The Odd Couple*. Prior to the start of a scheduled Mets-Pirates game, the teams pulled off a fake triple play for the sake of the cameras.

In the scene, sportswriter Oscar Madison, played by Walter Matthau, was in the press box when his roommate, Felix Unger, played by Jack Lemmon, phoned him and told him not to eat any hot dogs at the game because that's what they were having for dinner. Oscar was so involved in the phone call that he missed seeing baseball's most exciting play.

Moaned Oscar, "It's the first time I ever saw a triple play and didn't see it."

Nuttiest baseball contest run by a newspaper

Cincinnati Enquirer 1982

With the Reds already firmly entrenched in the cellar in July 1982, the *Cincinnati Enquirer* held a contest inviting readers to guess the date and time the team would be mathematically eliminated from the pennant race.

The winner received two tickets to the Reds' final home game of the season.

The runner-up got four tickets to the same game.

Highest annual salary for a player who was the recipient of a charity drive

$1.5 million
George Brett, Kansas City Royals 1990

All-Star George Brett—miffed that fellow superstars were signing contracts calling for annual salaries of $2 to $4 million—complained in a 1990 newspaper interview that he was underpaid.

Brett made $1.5 million for the season.

Feeling oh-so-sorry for Brett's slave wages, Kansas City radio station disc jockey Steve Douglas organized a mock charity drive "in recognition that a significant Royals player is down on his luck."

Douglas urged citizens to drop off clothing, canned goods, and even Kleenex (so Brett could wipe his eyes). One listener actually donated a gift certificate for maintenance on Brett's Mercedes.

Brett quickly got the point. He confessed to the press

that his salary complaint "was about the dumbest thing I've ever done."

Most times a player stuck a baseball in his mouth for a TV show

2 times
Rey Palacios, Kansas City Royals   1989

Royals utility man Rey Palacios has a big mouth. And to prove it, he stuffed a whole baseball in his mouth twice for the TV cameras.

In 1989, Palacios demonstrated his talent on a pregame show produced by the Home Sports Entertainment Network, a Dallas cable TV company.

"I didn't believe he could stick a baseball in his mouth, but he did it for our cameras," said producer Greg Maiuro. "Rey is the kind of guy who runs off at the mouth constantly and never shuts up. He said that when he was in the minors, his manager got fed up with his chatter and told him, 'Rey, just go stick a ball in your mouth and shut up.' So he did. And that's how Rey got started."

Costliest answer by a player to a *USA Today* poll

Mickey Mahler, Texas Rangers   1986

In 1986, *USA Today* asked Rangers hurler Mickey Mahler: "If you were baseball commissioner for a day, what one thing would you change about the game?"

Mahler responded: "Every player who has played three straight years in the majors, I'd send back to Triple A for one month just to let them see what it was like so they won't forget how good they have it now."

The very next day, Mahler was shipped out to the Rangers' Triple A farm club in Oklahoma City.

Longest string of "you knows" uttered while answering an interviewer's question

16 "you knows"
Mike Easler, Pittsburgh Pirates   1980

Outfielder Mike Easler rattled off 16 "you knows" in 29 seconds to set a, you know, record for overuse of the stock phrase.

During a taped interview in 1980, sportscaster Keith Olbermann asked Easler if his Pirates were in a slump. Easler, obviously a youknowversity graduate, gave this response:

"I think, you know (1), the guys are, you know (2), we're playing hard, you know (3), we're playing, you know (4), we're going out there and giving everything we've got. I know I am, and I know the other guys are, you know (5). It's just something, you know (6), you get guys that're hot like Matthews. He's swinging the bat real good this series, you know (7), and these guys have been throwing good ball games. You get a guy like Niekro, I mean, you know (8), they can pitch, you know (9), and these guys come against us, you know (10), they just love to knock off a pennant contender like us, you know (11), and, you know (12), they're just loosey-goosey, you know (13). They just go out there and just, you know (14), just try to bury us, you know (15), but the thing is, we're playing our type of baseball, you know (16), and the breaks have been going their way."

Biggest age difference between an actor and the ballplayer he portrayed

26 years
William Bendix, The Babe Ruth Story   *1948*

In one of the worst cases of miscasting in Hollywood history, actor William Bendix tried to pass himself off as a 16-year-old Babe Ruth—even though Bendix was a paunchy, middle-aged 42 at the time.

The actor said he knew agreeing to star in *The Babe Ruth Story* was a major mistake the moment he attended a preview in Los Angeles.

"In the early part of the picture, when I'm discovered in the orphanage, the scene was full of 16- and 17-year-old kids. Do I have a kid playing me? No, I have to do it with makeup! The audience laughed. I would have laughed, too, but I felt too bad."

In the film, Bendix wore a fake putty nose and had

to learn to bat and throw left-handed, but he wasn't very good at it. The movie was a staggering box-office flop and deserved the scathing reviews it received.

The Babe himself attended the New York premiere of the stinkeroo on July 26, 1948. Just three weeks later he died.

Oddballs and Ends
WARPED RECORDS THAT DIDN'T
FIT IN ANY OF THE
OTHER CATEGORIES

**Most hotel fires accidentally
started by a player in a season**

2 fires
Rudy York, Boston Red Sox–Chicago White Sox
1947

Rudy York found out the hard way that cigarettes can be hazardous to your health. While smoking, he accidentally set two hotel rooms aflame and nearly killed himself.

While a first baseman for the Red Sox, York lived in a Boston hotel. In the wee hours of the morning on April 26, 1947, a hotel guest smelled smoke and phoned the desk clerk. Hotel employees traced the smoke to the room where York was sleeping. They opened the door with a pass key, saw that the room was ablaze, awakened the player, and led him to safety. York was singed and had inhaled some smoke, but otherwise was not injured. Meanwhile, firemen quickly extinguished the flames and cited smoking in bed as the cause of the fire.

Four months later, on August 23rd, after he was traded to the White Sox, York's Chicago hotel room caught fire. Though he wasn't in the room at the time, Rudolph the red-faced first baseman got blamed for that blaze, too. Firemen officially listed the cause as "lighted cigarette left on window sill."

After Rudy retired the next year, he became—of all things—a fire prevention officer with the Georgia State Forestry Commission. His job: To spread the word that most fires are caused by carelessness!

Greatest distance from the dugout that a player was forced to sit because he smelled so bad

10 feet
Casey Stengel, Brooklyn Dodgers   1912

A close encounter with a smelly pig got Casey Stengel kicked off his own team's bench for an entire game.

Right after Stengel joined the Dodgers in 1912, the team went to New Jersey for an exhibition game. Before the game, players were invited to participate in a contest that paid $50 to the first person who could catch a pig smeared with foul-smelling axle grease. Stengel—

looking to make some quick money—enthusiastically joined in.

Casey chased after the slick porker, wrestled it to the ground, and wrapped himself around the squealing critter until the judges declared him the winner.

Elated, Stengel hustled to the bench $50 richer and ready to play. But his teammates took one whiff of his stinking uniform and roared: *"Pee-yew!"* They wouldn't let him near them. So Stengel was forced to sit on the ground 10 feet away from the dugout for the whole game.

Mighty Casey had stunk out.

Most bee invasions in a ballpark

3 invasions
Riverfront Stadium, Cincinnati   1976, 1980, 1987

The bee team took the field three times in 11 years at Cincinnati's Riverfront Stadium. People and players alike ran for cover as swarms of bees swept into the ballpark.

The first attack came on April 17, 1976, when a swarm took command of the visiting team's dugout and delayed the game for 30 minutes while players hid in the clubhouse until the all-clear was sounded.

Four years later the buzzing bees returned, but they merely clung to the backstop screen and quietly watched the game. The only people who were really annoyed were the fans who sat behind home plate, but they weren't about to shoo away the bees.

Invasion No. 3 came on May 10, 1987. This time so

many bees participated in the attack that three bee-keepers had to be called to clear the field.

While the roundup was taking place, one angry insect stung Cincinnati Reds pitcher Ted Power on the index finger of his pitching hand. But the sting didn't bother Power—he proceeded to strike out 11 batters that day for a career high.

Most outrageous message flashed on a scoreboard

Candlestick Park, San Francisco 1981

Even the many hearing-impaired people in the stands appreciated the laughter when this shameful greeting went up on the electronic scoreboard at San Francisco's Candlestick Park in 1981: THE GIANTS WELCOME THE CALIFORNIA SCHOOL FOR THE DEATH.

Longest ceremonial first pitch on Opening Day

150 feet
Roger Owens, Dodger Stadium, Los Angeles 1976

The Dodgers' nuttiest fan got the thrill of a lifetime in 1976 when he threw out the first ball to open the season.

Peanut vendor Roger Owens made his pitch from Dodger Stadium's second level, where he normally works, all the way to home plate 150 feet away.

And the seasoned salesman hurled a perfect toss to

catcher Steve Yeager. In fact, Owens's throw was so on-target that Yeager never even had to move his glove.

Owens's fantastic feat was no surprise to Dodgers fans who had watched him toss 1½-ounce bags of peanuts with astounding accuracy for years. The vendor, who billed himself as "The Peanut Man," easily hit fans' hands with throws overhand, underhand, behind his back, and between his legs.

In a tribute to his popularity among fans, the Dodgers let him throw out the first ball of the 1976 season.

It was an honor usually reserved for top politicians and Hall of Famers . . . so Owens made history not only by throwing the longest Opening Day pitch, but by becoming the first vendor ever to toss out a first ball.

Owens estimates that over the past 33 years he's thrown a staggering 2½ million bags of peanuts—with "no peanut elbow developed yet."

Most players to display sparklers at a game

12 players
New York Yankees 1960

After flamboyant Chicago White Sox owner Bill Veeck installed a Comiskey Park scoreboard that exploded when the home team belted a homer, some opposing teams considered it bush.

The Yankees came up with their own clever way of celebrating a New York homer. Bob Fishel of the Yankees' publicity department slipped New York manager Casey Stengel a dozen sparklers to use in the dugout in the event of a Yankee round-tripper at Comiskey Park.

When Mickey Mantle clouted a homer—and the partisan Veeck scoreboard remained silent—a dozen of his teammates lit sparklers and paraded around the dugout.

For the Yankees, it was a sparkling way of showing up Bill Veeck.

Most times a Triple Crown winner was denied MVP honors

2 times
Ted Williams, Boston Red Sox   1942, 1947

Twice Red Sox slugger Ted Williams led the American League in batting, home runs, and runs batted in—yet both times he failed to win the MVP award.

It didn't help matters that he didn't get along with many sportswriters—including some of the very same ones who got to select the Most Valuable Player.

In 1942, Williams hit .356, belted 36 homers, and drove in 137 runs. But the sportswriters cast their ballots for Joe Gordon, the second baseman for the pennant-winning New York Yankees. Gordon finished the year fourth in batting (.322), sixth in homers (18), and fourth in RBIs (103).

Five years later, in 1947, Williams once again won the Triple Crown, batting .343, clubbing 32 homers, and knocking in 114 runs. Yet he lost out to Yankees superstar Joe DiMaggio who was seventh in hitting (.315), sixth in homers (20), and third in RBIs (97).

Amazingly, Williams did win the MVP award in 1946—after finishing *second* in batting (.342), homers (38), and RBIs (123)!

Most runs nullified by an umpire

4 runs
Jim McKean, American League   1976

First-base umpire Jim McKean became a legend in his own time-out when he nullified a game-winning grand slam.

The New York Yankees were leading Milwaukee, 9–6, when the Brewers staged a rally in the bottom of the ninth inning and loaded the bases. As Don Money came up to bat, New York manager Billy Martin began frantically waving to his players to reposition themselves.

First baseman Chris Chambliss saw Martin's gestures and asked McKean for time. The umpire called time a split second before relief pitcher Dave Pagan threw the ball. Money then belted the pitch into the left-field bleachers for what appeared to be a grand slam, giving the Brewers a stunning 10–9 victory.

Milwaukee County Stadium went wild and many of the jubilant Brewers ran into the clubhouse, thinking they had won. Through the happy din, McKean waved his arms and ruled that since he had called time, he had to disallow all four runs.

Money glumly returned to the batter's box. This time he hit a sacrifice fly and the Brewers ended up losing, 9–7. His grand slam had only been a four-runner to defeat.

Biggest differential in distance between a homer hit down the line and one hit to straightaway center field

226 feet
Polo Grounds, New York   1911–1963

No stadium had more bizarre dimensions than the Polo Grounds, the long-time home of the New York Giants.

Pull hitters had a field day. The left-field foul pole was only 279 feet away, while the right-field wall was even closer—a mere pop-fly-swatting 257 feet from home plate.

But the bane for batters was center field. It was so far away it seemed to cross a couple of time zones—an incredible 483 feet from home.

The difference between walloping a homer to straightaway center field and one to right field was a whopping 226 feet!

Recalled the Giants' left-handed-hitting outfielder Dusty Rhodes, who played in the Polo Grounds from 1952 to 1957, "You either pulled the ball 260 feet and got a cheap homer or you hit it 480 feet straight away and wound up with nothing more than an out."

Most players ever to try to use chipped beef to win a game

22 players
New York Giants 1933

Giants second baseman Hughie Critz was so superstitious he once convinced his whole team to eat creamed chipped beef for breakfast. He was certain it would bring them luck on the field. It didn't.

During the 1933 season, the Giants were having trouble hitting the ball. But one afternoon they unexpectedly shelled the Cincinnati Reds, scoring 14 runs and banging out 19 hits. Critz then tried to find out why his team had suddenly come alive at the plate.

He took a poll of teammates, asking what they'd had for breakfast the morning of the game. He discovered that most had chowed down on creamed chipped beef.

"That's it!" Critz whooped. "Anything that can help us score 14 runs ought to be something we take seriously!"

He talked all his teammates into breakfasting on creamed chipped beef before their next game, against the Pittsburgh Pirates. The result? The Giants lost, 6–5.

Creamed chipped beef—obviously not the breakfast of champions—was crossed off the Giants' menu.

Most times one game was played

3 times
New York Yankees vs. Detroit Tigers   1932

The New York Yankees and Detroit Tigers tangled in a game that had to be played over and over again.

Problems started in the second inning of the 1932 game when the Yankees' Tony Lazzeri batted fifth, as he had done for some time. Umpire Dick Nallin told him that the team's official lineup card listed him as the sixth batter. New York manager Joe McCarthy hurriedly explained that he had made a mistake in filling out the lineup card, and asked the umpire to let Lazzeri bat in his usual fifth slot.

Nallin agreed. But as soon as Lazzeri hit a single, Tigers manager Bucky Harris lodged a protest—saying the umpire had no right to change the lineup in mid-game.

Nallin ignored him and yelled, "Play ball!" When the Yankees won, 6–3, Harris filed a protest with American League President William Harridge.

The president ordered the game replayed. A month later, the two teams met again. But the game ended in a 7–7 tie when it was called on account of darkness.

The game was replayed again the following day. This time Detroit came out on top, 4–1, in a victory that took three games to win.

Most expensive sunglasses ever bought by a player

$3,500
Kevin Mitchell, San Francisco Giants   1987

Flamboyant outfielder Kevin Mitchell wanted sunglasses a shade better than all the rest, so the extravagant Giant shelled out $3,500 for a gaudy pair trimmed in diamonds.

And just in case 1989's National League MVP misplaced those preposterous peeper protectors, Mitchell paid another $500 for a backup pair.

Most "infantile" scoreboard message

Dodger Stadium, Los Angeles   1969

The New York Mets were playing the Dodgers in Los Angeles when Mets outfielder Ron Swoboda's wife, Cecilia, gave birth to the couple's first child back in New York. Because of the three-hour time difference between the coasts, it was 10 P.M. Friday night on the field, but already 1 A.M. Saturday morning at the hospital.

The Dodgers relayed the happy news to Swoboda via this "timely" scoreboard message: CONGRATULATIONS, RON SWOBODA. YOUR NEW SON WAS BORN TOMORROW MORNING.

Most consecutive games played before demanding: "Bench me or trade me!"

4 games
George Thomas, Boston Red Sox   1967

If nothing else, Red Sox utilityman George Thomas was consistent. No matter which position he played, he never failed to drive Boston manager Dick Williams nuts.

That's why Thomas usually took the field only in an emergency. But he was such a fun-loving flake he didn't care—he enjoyed sitting on the bench and making his teammates laugh.

During the 1967 season, Thomas finally got a chance to play in left field. He was mediocre in his first game, but to the player's surprise, Williams left him there.

Another game passed, then a third and a fourth, and Thomas was still in left field. It was lonely out there —he missed cutting up with his pals back in the dugout.

So after the fourth game, Thomas issued this ultimatum to the Red Sox' front office: "Bench me or trade me!"

They benched him.

Longest game delay caused by a bug invasion

38 minutes
Toronto Blue Jays vs. Milwaukee Brewers   1990

A mind-boggling invasion of flying bugs had players swatting gnats and mosquitoes instead of hits at Toronto's SkyDome. The invasion was so annoying that the pesky swarm forced the umpires to stop the game.

Dive-bombing and biting, the horde from hell also included flying ants, midges, and moths. The buzzing brood formed such a thick assemblage that they looked like clouds of smoke covering the field.

"I've seen games called by rain, wind, and snow, but never by bugs," said exasperated umpire Don Denkinger, who halted the game between the Blue Jays and Brewers for 38 minutes.

Players were used to seeing pop flies—but now they were also seeing mom flies. The bugs were swarming because it was their mating season, explained a pest control expert.

Stadium engineers finally drove the love bugs away by closing the SkyDome's retractable roof and turning up the air conditioning. That cooled off the insects' ardor pronto and let the players get on with the game.

That wasn't the first time players had been bugged. On June 2, 1959, a game between the Baltimore Orioles and Chicago White Sox at Comiskey Park was delayed nearly half an hour by a swarm of gnats.

Groundskeepers tried bug sprays and torches, but failed to clear the field. Finally, a fireworks display for a postgame show was hauled in from beyond center field. A smoke bomb was set off, and soon the pesky flies no longer ruled the field.

Longest putt ever made in the bullpen during a game

40 feet
Steve Nicosia, Pittsburgh Pirates 1979

To while away the time until they were called into the game, the Pirates' relief corps used to play miniature golf in the bullpen.

They laid out a course and dug holes in the dirt and even had little flags. They used baseballs for golf balls and a bat for a putter.

But one night at Dodger Stadium, catcher Steve Nicosia and the bullpen gang seemed more concerned about birdies and pars than balls and strikes. "I'm playing with [pitcher] Don Robinson and I've got a 40-foot putt, over the pitcher's mound, to win," recalled Steve. "I make it, and I go crazy. I'm pumping my arms and they're giving me high fives."

But what he didn't know was that the TV cameras had caught him golfing and a replay of his long putt was broadcast back in Pittsburgh. When Nicosia returned home, he was called into the general manager's office for a dressing down. "That," recalled Nicosia, "was the end of the golf."

Most runs scored in a game that was called for lack of balls

36 runs
Cincinnati Reds vs. Boston Red Sox   1938

When a monster dust storm struck during an exhibition game between Cincinnati and Boston, the players didn't have the balls to continue—because every fly ball hit into the fierce wind was blown far away and lost.

The supply of balls was exhausted by the eighth inning, so the umpire called the game with the score tied, 18–18.

The high winds in Florence, South Carolina, where the game was played, were responsible for most of those 36 runs. Each time a player smacked a fly ball, it took a crazy, zigzag flight. For instance, balls hit far into left field made a detour in midair and shot over the right fielders' heads and out of the park. Foul balls sailed more than a block away from the stadium. Miraculously, no one was hurt by the wind-driven projectiles.

Gutsiest hotfoot ever given by a player

Moe Drabowsky, Kansas City Royals   1969

Moe Drabowsky never set the world on fire as a pitcher—but he did come chillingly close to sending the baseball commissioner's shoes up in flames.

Fun-loving Moe gave Bowie Kuhn a memorable hotfoot as Moe's former team, the Baltimore Orioles, celebrated their American League Championship Series triumph over the Minnesota Twins in 1969.

Drabowsky, whom Baltimore had traded to the Kansas City Royals the year before, walked into the winners' clubhouse to extend congratulations to his old buddies. That's when he spotted Commissioner Kuhn —the perfect target for a prank, thought Drabowsky. While Kuhn was happily occupied with the trophy presentation, mischievous Moe crawled up behind him and sprayed lighter fluid around his shoes—then set it on fire.

Players snickered but Kuhn was blissfully unaware at first that anything was wrong. He finally paid attention when the blaze spread to his brand-new shoes. The commissioner leaped like a pivot man on a double play and quickly stomped out the flames before any damage was done.

Marveled Moe, "He must have jumped four or six feet. Yowww! What a scream he gave out. The best part was he never figured out who did it."

Longest hunger strike by a pitcher's brother who wouldn't eat until the hurler won again

17 days
Frank Slaton   1986

After California Angels starting pitcher Jim Slaton saw his season record plunge from 4–1 to 4–6 in 1986, his brother Frank vowed not to eat any solid food until Jim won again.

Unfortunately, after a couple of weeks, Jim still hadn't broken into the win column and was demoted to the bullpen. So Frank amended his vow, telling Jim, "Make it a win or a save."

According to Jim, Frank even tried to talk their father into joining his hunger strike. But wise old Dad responded, "I love my son, but I'm not crazy!"

Frank began his hunger strike on June 13th. He ended it on June 30th—that's when his brother was released without ever winning another game for the Angels.

Jim's loss wasn't his brother's gain. Frank shed 16 pounds on his wacky fast.

Costliest cab ride taken by a future Hall of Famer

$1,000
Babe Ruth, New York Yankees 1925

After a wild night of boozing, Babe Ruth wisely took a taxi home—but he unwisely goofed and paid the cabbie a small fortune for hauling him only a few blocks.

The Sultan of Swat had been knocking down drinks at a thirst-quenching pace before hailing the cab in downtown Manhattan. When Ruth arrived in front of his apartment, he staggered out of the taxi and the driver growled: "That's two bucks, pal."

Ruth fumbled around in his pocket, handed the cabbie what he thought was a $10 bill, and boomed, "Keep the change." The cabbie's jaw dropped as he stared at the bill. Then he hastily stuffed it in his pocket and roared away.

It wasn't until Ruth got indoors that he learned he'd really been taken for a ride. With John Barleycorn clouding his vision, he'd unwittingly given the driver a $1,000 bill!

In recalling his tale of woe, Ruth said ruefully, "I'd better look at my money a little more carefully before I spend it."

Most strikes erased from the count by an umpire

2 strikes
Ed Hurley, American League 1959

Two strikes against Boston Red Sox hitter Frank Malzone were wiped out because an umpire wasn't paying attention.

During a 1959 game in Detroit, the Red Sox third baseman had fouled off a pitch from Tigers hurler Paul Foytack and had taken a called strike.

That's when first-base umpire Ed Hurley got into the act. Hurley yelled, "Wait a minute! I didn't see it!" Moments earlier, he had gone out to the Boston bullpen to chew out a player for riding the umpires. When Hurley turned around, there were two strikes on Malzone.

"He told Joe Paparella, the plate umpire, the strikes didn't count because he hadn't been ready to call a play at first base," recalled Malzone. "Paparella wanted to leave at least one strike on the board, but Hurley said no. So the count went back to 0-and-0 on me. And Foytack was burning up!"

The next pitch from the fuming Foytack was a slider—and Malzone walloped it for a home run. Chuckled Malzone, "I've always given Hurley credit for that one."

Only player to hit a fungo that postponed a game

Frank Thomas, Chicago Cubs   1960

The Chicago Cubs and Milwaukee Braves played in a fog before Frank Thomas's fungo hit convinced umpires that the outfielders risked getting beaned by an unseen fly ball.

When the 1960 game at Milwaukee's County Stadium got underway, a thick fog blew in from Lake Michigan. The two teams managed to play 4½ innings of scoreless baseball without anyone getting hurt or losing the ball in the fog.

But then the men in blue had second thoughts and wondered if they were tempting fate.

They called time and walked out to center field, where they joined the three Chicago outfielders. They then had Cubs player Frank Thomas, who was not in the game, stand at home plate and hit a fly ball to center with a fungo bat. When neither the umps nor the outfielders could see the ball, the game was called.

Said Thomas, "The only way we could have continued was if the ball had a miniature foghorn inside."

Most letters in the name of a major league player

45 letters
Alan Mitchell Edward George Patrick Henry
Gallagher, San Francisco Giants–California Angels
1970–1973

Third baseman Al Gallagher's full name stretched a tongue-twisting 45 letters—nearly twice as many as there are in the entire alphabet!

With a choice of six first and middle names to choose from, teammates could've nicknamed him Al, Mitch, Ed, George, Pat, or Hank. Instead they just called him "Dirty Al" for short.

But they didn't call him that for long, because his big-league career fizzled after only four years.

Gallagher had his father to blame for giving him a name that took almost a whole ball game to say and, on paper, looked like a page out of the Manhattan telephone directory. His dad had wanted six sons and picked their names in advance. But it took so long for the first one to arrive that impatient Papa stuck son No. 1 with all half-dozen names!

Gallagher's full name holds the major league record as the longest by only one letter. An infielder who played with the St. Louis Cardinals from 1914 to 1918 bore the tongue-tiring monicker Christian Frederick Albert John Henry David Betzel. As a public service to those who knew him, he went by the nickname "Bruno."

Longest span of indecision by umpires before making a call

28 minutes
Substitute Umpires 1979

The umpires in a 1979 San Francisco Giants–New York Mets game belonged on a playground, not a major league diamond. They seesawed back and forth for nearly half an hour before finally making a decision.

Brought in as substitute arbiters during the umpires' strike that year, the bumbling bozos in blue reversed themselves twice as the players and a Shea Stadium crowd steamed over the holdup.

The charade began when Mets batter Lee Mazzilli hit a fly to Giants outfielder Jack Clark, who caught the ball and then dropped it while drawing back to make the throw. Mets runner Frank Taveras, who was on third, scored. But Richie Hebner, on first, wasn't sure if the ball had been caught and was tagged out between first and second base.

Umpire Phil Lospitalier ruled it a double play—which brought Mets manager Joe Torre storming out for a scream-fest. The three other umps huddled with Lospitalier, and after five minutes, he reversed the call.

That brought Giants manager Joe Altobelli onto the field shrieking that the umps were incompetent. Under assault from all sides, the quartet then ran under the stands to puzzle over what to do.

When they came out, the umps announced a Solomonlike decision: Mazzilli was out because the ball had been caught, but Hebner was safe on first because he had been confused by the umpire.

"Even Little League umpires could have done a better job than these jokers," fumed Torre.

Most tree branches used to break a
losing streak

4 branches
Jim Deshaies, Houston Astros 1988

After the Astros dropped 11 straight games in July 1988, pitcher Jim Deshaies decided a bad spell had been cast on the club.

So he bought a book on black magic, boned up on ways to break spells—and went out on a limb to help his team.

When he showed up for the next game, which was against the San Diego Padres, the superstitious hurler brought four tree branches to the park. Deshaies broke them, spit on them, mumbled some mumbo-jumbo, and then burned the limbs.

What the devil? asked his teammates. But to everyone's surprise, the Astros conjured up a victory.

Longest distance a player spat tobacco juice
into a spittoon

25 feet
Thad Tillotson, New York Yankees 1967

Yankees pitcher Thad Tillotson wowed teammates with his accuracy—not with his fastball, but with his tobacco spitting.

When the tobacco-chewing chucker first showed up in the Yankees' dressing room in 1967, he raised a few eyebrows by bringing with him his own spittoon. They soon learned to look both ways before walking by his locker because he was always spitting into it.

Tillotson was a long-distance spitter. As onlookers watched in amazement in the clubhouse, Tillotson consistently launched tobacco juice high in the air only to hit the spittoon from across the room.

"Best accuracy I've ever seen from 25 feet away," remarked astounded manager Ralph Houk, a Beech-Nut connoisseur himself for years.

Unfortunately, Houk quickly discovered Tillotson was a much better spitter than a pitcher. In his two years in the majors, both with the Yankees, Tillotson sported a record of 4–9. He wasn't as good as Houk had expectorated.

Longest sacrifice fly

435 miles
Joe Altobelli, New York Yankees 1986

Believe it or not, Yankees coach Joe Altobelli once swatted a sacrifice fly that traveled from Cleveland to Milwaukee 435 miles away!

Joe was snoozing in a Cleveland hotel following a road game when he was awakened in the morning by a large winged insect that was dive-bombing his face. He swatted it away, but minutes later the pesky bug returned.

The coach waved it off, but seconds later the bug was back. Wide awake by then, Joe packed his suitcase and joined his team for its trip to Milwaukee.

When Joe's suitcase arrived late that night at a Milwaukee hotel, he opened it—and to his shock, out flew the Bug from Hell!

Joe grabbed a magazine and hammered the insect into oblivion to record a one-of-its-kind "sacrifice fly."

Most embarrassing ballpark flag-burning

Veterans Stadium, Philadelphia 1990

In the birthplace of American independence, tens of thousands of Veterans Stadium spectators helplessly watched the Stars and Stripes burn to a crisp.

And the Phillies were unwittingly to blame.

In an early celebration of the Fourth of July in 1990, the team set off fireworks after a night game. But fallout from one of the pyrotechnics accidentally ignited an American flag that was fluttering 50 feet above the stands in center field. The Red, White, and Blue went up in a blaze of Old Glory.

Red-faced club officials replaced the flag by dawn's early light.

Longest one-player strike over dirty pants

4 games
Yank Robinson, St. Louis Browns 1889

A dispute over soiled trousers prompted Browns second baseman Yank Robinson to stage a four-game sit-down strike.

Just before a May 2, 1889, game, Yank discovered his pants were dirty. Since it was Ladies Day at the ballpark, he was embarrassed to be seen in anything but a sparkling-clean uniform. So Robinson sent a boy from the bleachers to get a pair of pants owned by his teammate, Tip O'Neill, who had an extra uniform at his apartment across the street.

But despite Robinson's note authorizing the boy admittance to the park, a surly old gatekeeper wouldn't let the youngster back inside. As a result, Yank had to play in the dirty pants. After the game, he chewed out the gatekeeper, and got slapped with a $25 fine by Browns owner Chris von der Ahe.

The next day, the Browns were set to travel to Kansas City for a four-game series. But Yank refused to go unless the fine was lifted—and all but one of his teammates sided with him. When the train pulled out, a rookie was the only player aboard!

Yank finally convinced the St. Louis players it was his fight alone, and talked them into taking a later train. But Robinson's strike had a demoralizing effect on the Browns. They lost three of their four games with Kansas City.

Realizing the seriousness of the situation, nervous owner von der Ahe finally agreed that Yank wouldn't have to pay the $25 fine. Yank ended his four-game strike that day and led his team to a 21–0 victory— putting them back in the victory column by the seat of his (clean) pants.

Fewest people to get wet before a rain delay was called

3 people
Toronto Skydome 1989

A 1989 game between the visiting Milwaukee Brewers and the Toronto Blue Jays momentarily was halted by rain because the batter, catcher, and plate umpire were the only ones getting wet.

With the forecast calling for clear skies, SkyDome

officials had opened the brand-new stadium's rollaway top. But in the fifth inning, a sudden storm hit.

"We started closing the roof, but we didn't have much experience at that point in how long it would take to close it," recalled Blue Jays spokesman Howard Starkman.

"The last place where it was still open was the space above home plate. The other players stayed dry as the roof closed over them, but the umpire, batter, and catcher were getting soaked.

"The umpire called a rain delay and the three of them ran for cover. It took about eight minutes for the roof to finish closing.

"The funniest thing was that if the umpire had stepped back two feet before calling the game, he would've been out of the rain!"

Longest time a player claimed to have overslept

3 days
Claudell Washington, Chicago White Sox   1978

When the Texas Rangers traded outfielder Claudell Washington to the White Sox for Bobby Bonds in 1978, Claudell didn't show up until four days after the transaction.

No one knew where he was the previous three days. When he finally found his new club, Claudell was asked why it took him so long to report. He replied, "I overslept."

Longest brawl after a hockey player threw out the first ball

10 minutes
Pittsburgh Pirates vs. Montreal Expos   1988

NHL superstar Mario Lemieux went to the ballpark and a hockey fight broke out.

The star center for the Pittsburgh Penguins tossed out the first ball on Amateur Hockey Night at Three Rivers Stadium before the game between the Pirates and Expos.

The NHL all-star obviously had some bizarre effect on the ballplayers. In the third inning, after giving up a two-run homer, Pirates hurler John Smiley hit batter Hubie Brooks in the back with a pitch. Brooks charged the mound and landed a couple of punches, triggering a bench-clearing brawl that lasted 10 minutes.

Pirates catcher Mike LaValliere, a former hockey player himself, wound up the only casualty when the pile of humanity met at the mound and collapsed on him. He left the game with muscle spasms.

"In hockey, you get to square off one-on-one," said LaValliere. "Man, we could have used Lemieux out there."

Meanwhile, the instigators of the fight, Brooks and Smiley, were ejected.

Observed Pirates pitcher Bob Walk, "What do you expect when a hockey player throws out the first pitch?"

The hottest prank ever pulled by a team trainer on a player

Frank Bowman, New York Giants 1948

Giants trainer Frank Bowman had a blazing good time pulling a joke on first baseman Johnny Mize in 1948.

Mize came into the trainer's room after a heavy workout, took off his sweatshirt, and went to get a drink of water. Bowman quickly soaked the shirt with alcohol.

When Mize returned, Bowman asked, "How are you feeling?"

"I feel tired but good," Mize replied.

"Better stay away from that hard liquor, John," cautioned Bowman. "That's what really knocks you out."

"What do you mean?" asked Mize. "I just had a couple of beers last night."

"Sure John, that's what they all say," replied the trainer. "But you can't fool me. Here, I'll prove it to you."

Bowman then lit a match and dropped it on Mize's alcohol-soaked sweatshirt. It burst into flames. "That's the alcohol you sweated out," said Bowman, trying hard to keep a straight face.

Mize, red-faced and perplexed, stamped out the fire. "Doc," he pleaded, "promise me you won't say anything about this to anyone."

Heaviest umpire in major league history

357 pounds
Eric Gregg, National League 1980

The running joke around the National League in 1980 was that you could always tell when and where Eric Gregg was umpiring. If the field sloped toward home plate, he was calling balls and strikes. If the diamond tilted toward the left, he was umpiring at third.

There was simply too much of Gregg to ignore. When he reached the bigs in 1976, he weighed 205 pounds. By the end of the 1980 season, the 6-foot-3-inch, 29-year-old umpire had beefed up to a whopping 357 pounds—the most of any major league arbiter ever.

"I developed a lot of bad eating habits," recalled Gregg. "I ate a lot of junk food and felt obliged to eat all the food that was served to me.

"The ribbing by players and fans became fierce. I was called 'Tons of Fun' and also 'Rerun,' named after a fat black kid on the TV show 'What's Happening?'"

After the 1980 season, Gregg realized he was eating himself out of a job and threatening his health. With the help of a trainer for the Philadelphia Phillies, Gregg went on a strict diet and exercised daily. By spring training of 1981, the ump had lost over 100 pounds.

Recalled Gregg, "The best part was that the players started calling me Eric again."

Most people needed to chase a pigeon off the field in a World Series game

8 people
New York Giants vs. Washington Senators 1933

The third game of the 1933 World Series got off to a flying stop when a plucky pigeon plopped down on the field—forcing a halt to the action as umpires and players tried to get the birdbrain out of the way.

With the New York Giants at bat, a blue pigeon landed right in front of Washington Senators shortstop Joe Cronin.

"Time!" shouted Cronin, who tried to shoo the bird away. But the pigeon gave him a dirty look and stood its ground.

Two umpires ran over and tried to thumb the bird out of the game. It ignored them by simply flying a few feet away.

Cronin, four teammates, two umpires, and even a Giants base runner chased after the pigeon—which scurried ahead of them on the ground and then doubled back by flying over their heads and alighting on the same spot from which it had just been chased.

In the stands, thousands of fans—including President Franklin D. Roosevelt—were doubled over with laughter.

After a five-minute delay, the feathered intruder finally fluttered into the air, circled the infield, and soared out of the ballpark.

Thundered Cronin later, "He was tramping around as if he owned the place!"

Most times played on losing All-Star teams

9 times
Carlton Fisk, American League   1972, 1973, 1976,
1977, 1978, 1980, 1981, 1982, 1985

Through two decades of All-Star appearances, veteran catcher Carlton Fisk never once got to celebrate with the winning team.

Fisk represented the Boston Red Sox in the showcase games of 1972, 1973, 1976, 1977, 1978, and 1980. But the American League All-Stars were defeated every single time.

Even changing Sox didn't help. After Fisk was traded to the Chicago White Sox, he was on the American League All-Star team in the 1981, 1982, and 1985 classics. They dropped all three contests.

When informed of the dubious record, American Leaguer Reggie Jackson reportedly quipped, "If the American League wants to win so badly, maybe Fisk should be traded to the National League."

Longest time a player watched an All-Star Game in the nude

10 minutes
Jackie Brandt, Baltimore Orioles   1961

Wacky Jackie Brandt got plenty of exposure at one of the 1961 All-Star games. He watched part of the action totally naked!

It was really all so innocent, according to Brandt, who played briefly in the midseason classic held at Candlestick Park in San Francisco.

"I had pinch-hit and was out of the game, so I went in the clubhouse to shower," recalled the Orioles' outfielder.

"But I wanted to watch the game and couldn't see it too good from the clubhouse. So I just wandered out in the runway leading from the clubhouse while I was drying off. I wasn't out there very long—just long enough to see a half-inning.

"It didn't seem like any big deal to me at the time —but apparently it did to a lot of other people." Especially the fans who spotted him in his birthday suit.

Costliest game of catch

*Earl Torgeson, Floyd Robinson, Chicago White Sox
1960*

White Sox hurler Early Wynn lost a heartbreaker
thanks to teammates Earl Torgeson and Floyd
Robinson—who weren't even in the game.

The Sox were trailing the Baltimore Orioles, 3–1, in
the top of the eighth inning at Memorial Stadium when
Chicago pinch hitter Ted Kluszewski slammed a three-
run homer.

But the runs were all erased from the scoreboard . . . because third-base umpire Ed Hurley had
called time a split second before the pitch.

Hurley's action had come after Orioles third baseman Brooks Robinson spotted Torgeson, Chicago's veteran first baseman, and the other Robinson, a rookie
outfielder, tossing a ball by the Sox bullpen in foul
territory. Brooks told the ump, "They're supposed to
be warming up inside the bullpen, Ed, not outside."

Hurley agreed and called time, but Orioles hurler
Milt Pappas didn't hear him and threw the gopher ball
that didn't count. Kluszewski was ordered to bat again,
and this time he lined out to center for the inning's
third out.

The Orioles held onto their lead—and Early Wynn
lost a game he should have won.

Worst winning percentage of a
team hypnotist

.242
Dr. David Tracy, St. Louis Browns 1950

After failing to win at least 60 games in each of the previous three seasons, the Browns were so desperate they hired New York psychologist-hypnotist Dr. David Tracy.

His job was to hypnotize the team into winners.

After a few sessions, Tracy announced that the club suffered from "losers' syndrome." Being traded to the Browns was the psychological equivalent of being shipped to Siberia, he said, adding that new players arrived in a dejected frame of mind. Fans and players—none of whom had psychology degrees—already knew this.

Nevertheless, the "whammy man," as the press called him, put players in a trance and told them such things as, "You will win . . . you will hit the ball with great power . . . you will hate the opposing pitchers. . . ."

The result? The Browns played like they were in a trance.

By May 31st the club had won just 8, lost 25, sported a woeful winning percentage of .242, and were mired in the American League cellar. And on that day Dr. Tracy was told, "You will seek other employment."

WHO ELSE BELONGS IN THE BASEBALL HALL OF SHAME'S WARPED RECORD BOOK?

Do you have any suggestions for new entries that belong in *The Baseball Hall of Shame's Warped Record Book*?

If you have information about a record that tops any that we have in this book, or of a dubious achievement that we neglected to include, please let us know. Here's your opportunity to pay a lighthearted tribute to the game we all love.

Please describe the new records in detail. Those that are documented with the greatest number of facts, such as first-hand accounts, newspaper and magazine clippings, or box scores, have the best chance of being included in a future *Warped Record Book*.

All submitted material becomes the property of The Baseball Hall of Shame and is nonreturnable. Mail your new records to:

The Baseball Hall of Shame
P.O. Box 31867
Palm Beach Gardens, FL 33420